Detecting and Combating
Malicious Email

Detecting and Combating Malicious Email

Julie JCH Ryan
Cade Kamachi

ELSEVIER

AMSTERDAM • BOSTON • HEIDELBERG
LONDON • NEW YORK • OXFORD • PARIS
SAN DIEGO • SAN FRANCISCO
SINGAPORE • SYDNEY • TOKYO

SYNGRESS.

Syngress is an Imprint of Elsevier

Acquiring Editor: Steve Elliot
Editorial Project Manager: Benjamin Rearick
Project Manager: Paul Prasad Chandramohan
Designer: Mark Rogers

Syngress is an imprint of Elsevier
225 Wyman Street, Waltham, MA 02451, USA

British Library Cataloguing-in-Publication Data
A catalogue record for this book is available from the British Library

Library of Congress Cataloging-in-Publication Data
A catalog record for this book is available from the Library of Congress

ISBN: 978-0-12-800110-3

For information on all Syngress publications
visit our website at http://store.elsevier.com/syngress

Working together
to grow libraries in
developing countries

www.elsevier.com • www.bookaid.org

TABLE OF CONTENTS

This book is for ordinary users who do not have deep technical knowledge about how computers and networks operate. It is written in plain language with the goal of providing you with enough knowledge to keep yourself safe from predators while not overwhelming you with technical details. It can be read easily from beginning to end, or each chapter can be individually considered. For those who are not interested in technical details, Chapter 4 can easily be skipped. For those who are not faced with management challenges, Chapter 6 can easily be skipped.

Chapter 1 introduces the concept of malicious messaging, providing context for the more detailed information provided in later chapters. The use of messaging systems for malicious purposes is not new: examples of the misuse of the mail range back to 1838. The challenge of recognizing and not falling victim to malicious messaging is discussed, as is the cleverness of the senders, who are motivated to convince recipients of the legitimacy of the messages.

Chapter 2 provides a detailed explanation of types of malicious messaging, with actual examples. The elements of the messages that provide indicators of the malicious nature are identified. This information is very useful in understanding how to detect and not fall victim to the attack.

Chapter 3 focuses on the motivations of the senders so that reverse psychology can be used as a defense. Understanding the psychology of malicious messaging can be as much of a resource to stopping it as any technology or security analysis. This is discussed in the context of the two primary goals of the attackers and how they go about trying to achieve those goals.

Chapter 4 is the most technical of all the chapters. It describes the structure of emails and tells you how to use that structure to as an aid to determining if a received message is malicious or benign. Elements in the headers, message body, and attachments are identified and discussed.

Chapter 5 is about the detection process. The process described can be applied to any detection challenge, but is presented in the context of malicious messaging detection efforts. The use of detection experience is also described to show you how you can use your experiences to improve your detection capabilities.

Chapter 6 is for those readers who are faced with the challenge of addressing the problem of malicious messaging for more than simply themselves. A framework for creating both defense in depth and defense in breadth for an enterprise is described. The framework addresses both the people and the technologies that can be used in these defenses.

Chapter 7 contains some final thoughts and recommendations. Since knowing what to do in case you fall victim is as important as knowing how to avoid danger in the first place, these thoughts can guide you through reaction and recovery.

For educators, this book can serve as a starting point for building awareness about dangers that lurk in electronic messaging. For managers, it can serve as a cornerstone to training programs designed to enhance corporate security and establishing safe computing behavior patterns. For parents, it can be of assistance in talking to children about the challenges associated with engaging in online communications.

AUTHOR BIOGRAPHIES

Julie Ryan is an Associate Professor at the George Washington University in Washington, DC, where she researches and teaches in the areas of information security, systems dynamics, and human–machine interactions. Dr. Ryan holds degrees of B.S. from the U.S. Air Force Academy, Master of Liberal Studies in Technology from Eastern Michigan University, and Doctor of Science from George Washington University. She is coauthor of "Defending Your Digital Assets Against Hackers, Crackers, Spies and Thieves" (2000) and editor of "Leading Issues in Information Warfare and Security."

Cade Kamachi holds a Computer Information Technology degree from Brigham Young University–Idaho as well as an MBA degree from Idaho State University. While at Idaho State University, he performed research and developed trainings as part of the National Information Assurance Training and Education Center (NIATEC). Cade has worked for both industry and government in technology and information-assurance roles that included duties from technical configurations to policy creation. He has aided in the creation and implementation of cyber security exercises for collegiate, industry, and government entities.

Corey Schou is a Fulbright Scholar, a frequent public speaker, an active researcher, and an author with more than 300 books, papers, articles, and other presentations. His interests include information assurance, risk management, software engineering, developing secure applications, security and privacy, and collaborative decision making.

He has been described in the press as the father of the knowledge base used worldwide to establish computer security and information assurance. He was responsible for compiling and editing computer security training standards for the U.S. government.

In 2003, he was selected as the first university professor at Idaho State University. He directs the Informatics Research Institute and the National Information Assurance Training and Education Center. His program was recognized by the U.S. government as a Center of Academic Excellence in Information Assurance and is a leading institution in the CyberCorps/Scholarship for Service program.

In addition to his academic accomplishments, he holds a broad spectrum of certifications including Certified Cyber Forensics Professional (CCFP), Certified Secure Software Lifecycle Professional (CSSLP), HealthCare Information Security and Privacy Practitioner (HCISPP), CISSP Information Systems Security Architecture Professional (CISSP-ISSAP), and CISSP Information Systems Security Management Professional (CISSP-ISSMP).

During his career, he has been recognized by many organizations including the Federal Information Systems Security Educators Association, which selected him as the 1996 Educator of the Year, and his research and center were cited by the Information Systems Security Association for Outstanding Contributions to the Profession. In 1997, he was given the TechLearn award for contributions to distance education.

He was nominated and selected as an honorary Certified Information Systems Security Professional (CISSP) based on his lifetime achievement. In 2001, the International Information Systems Security Certification Consortium (ISC)2 selected him as the second recipient of the Tipton award for contribution to the information security profession. In 2007, he was recognized a fellow of (ISC)2.

CHAPTER 1

Introduction

This book is about detecting and combatting malicious messaging, which is a mouthful and just a little overbearing in terms of language. In order to address this topic, we need to proceed in an orderly fashion, starting with defining what we mean by "'messaging," what we mean by "'malicious," what we mean by "detecting," and what we mean by "combating."

However, before we get to that, perhaps we should discuss why this topic is of interest and importance. The importance stems from consequences: what happens when malicious messaging is not detected, not thwarted, and is allowed to execute its planned improper behavior. That is in fact why we care. The consequences are theft of data, identity, money, intellectual property, rational opinion, and, at the most innocuous, theft of time. The various types of malicious messaging are designed to accomplish one or more of these thefts. As the value of the intended theft increases, the sophistication and planning associated with the malicious messaging increases. Even the least sophisticated effort can create relatively great harm to the target. Even if the harm is merely pennies in the greater scheme of things, if the "pennies" are yours, you do not want them stolen.

The point of this book is to give you the tools and knowledge you need to prevent the senders of malicious email from being able to steal from you. We will cover the various types of malicious emails, with examples; discuss the approaches to protecting yourself from these messages; explore the methods by which you can identify a potentially malicious message; and cover the methods by which you can combat malicious messages.

For those of you who are impatient and want the answers right up front, here is the executive summary of what to do to prevent problems:

1. Do not trust that any message you receive is legitimate: treat it with suspicion!

2. Use your eyes: look at the messages for content, misspellings, and other anomalies.
3. Do not click on any embedded links (unless you have to, and then use caution).
4. Do not open any attachments directly from email (there are safe ways to explore attachments).
5. Do not believe in fairy tales, get-rich-quick schemes, or conspiracy theories.
6. Keep your antivirus software up to date.

Obviously, this list of summary preventative recommendations is not carved in stone; you will occasionally need to open an attachment or follow a link. Nevertheless, there are safe ways to do that and ways that are not so safe.

We are all human; we make mistakes. What should you do if something does go wrong? This, unfortunately, is harder to summarize. It really very much depends on the nature of the problem, what system you are using, and how comfortable you feel with repairing your own system. If you do not know what the problem is, but you think something may have happened, here is a list of things to start with:

1. turn off your internet connection;
2. scan your system for malicious files, if you have the capability;
3. in the worst-case scenario, rebuild your system or take it to a trustworthy computer repair facility to have it scanned and repaired.

It is worth pointing out that at the instant a problem occurs, all of your files and data are suspect and may be corrupted. Prepare for problems by making sure you regularly make copies of your files, photos, and media. When a problem occurs, it is heartbreaking to lose the only copies of photos of dear friends, relatives, or events. Having known good backups in a safe place can help prevent that loss. From time to time, double-check your backup files to make sure they are usable.

A LITTLE HISTORY

It is important, and a bit comforting, to understand that the problem of bad guys using messaging technology for malicious purposes is not a new phenomenon. Packages and letters have been used for a very long time as conveyors of dangers. As the technology for messaging has evolved, so has the use of the technology: as methods have changed over time to accommodate new mailing methods and new packaging materials, the bad guys have modified their methods as well. Just to illustrate this point, here are a few historical notes.

1838: James Grant published "Sketches in London," part of which is devoted to exploring the growing problem of "begging impostors who ply their avocation by means of letters," one of whom was so successful as to net approximately 600 pounds per year.[1]

1978: Theodore Kaczynski had a 17-year career of sending bombs through the U.S. mail. He killed three and injured 24 people, terrifying many more in the process. His mail bombs were malicious indeed, made to explode when opened.[2]

2001: Letters containing anthrax were mailed to various U.S. government offices and news outlets, resulting in five deaths, numerous infections, and a massive disruption to the U.S. Postal System as measures were put in place to neutralize any remaining contaminants.[3]

2013: Letters containing traces of ricin, a potent poison, were sent to several U.S. government offices. The letters were detected prior to causing harm, and were later traced to a man who sent the letters to exact revenge on an enemy.[4]

These four examples show the use of the postal system to conduct malicious activity—ranging from fraud to murder—by nefarious persons is evident. There are more examples to be found for those who like to study history.

---

[1] Grant, James. Sketches in London. 1838 Available online at http://www.victorianlondon. org/publications/sketchesinlondon-1a.htm.

[2] There is a wealth of material regarding what became known as the Unabomber available in many different venues. A nice summary can be found on the FBI website, http://www.fbi.gov/news/stories/2008/april/unabomber_042408, in the story titled "FBI 100: The Unabomber", posted April 24, 2008.

[3] The FBI website contains links to comprehensive reporting on the investigation: "Amerithrax or Antrax Investigation", http://www.fbi.gov/about-us/history/famous-cases/anthrax-amerithrax/amerithrax-investigation.

[4] The FBI website contains a series of reports on this case, including the press release announcing the guilty plea by the perpetrator. http://www.fbi.gov/jackson/press-releases/2014/mississippi-man-pleads-guilty-in-ricin-letter-investigation

In addition to these specific examples, it is not uncommon to be overwhelmed with catalogs near the holidays, lottery solicitations offering recipients both magazine subscriptions and a chance to win a large amount of money, and fraudulent invoices sent with the hope that the recipient will simply pay the bill without checking to ensure its legitimacy. Postal mail is filled with scams, which is one of the reasons the U.S. Postal Code defines the use of the postal system in commission of a crime as a separate crime itself. The U.S. Postal Service helpfully provides a list of activities that can potentially result in charges of mail fraud; these include "illegal sweepstakes schemes, chain letters, travel and vacation scams, merchandise misrepresentations, phony billings, fraudulent investment opportunities, work-at-home schemes, rebate fraud, and foreign lottery scams."[5]

These activities, and other criminal actions, have transitioned seamlessly to electronically networked communications. Junk faxes clog facsimile machines and waste paper. Unsolicited bulk email, also known as unsolicited commercial email or spam, may appear to cause less environmental damage, since little paper is involved, but does clog bandwidth and costs both service providers and consumers in electricity and bandwidth, as well as time. The problem has attracted so much attention that laws have been passed in the US at both the local and federal levels limiting or banning such email, and the Federal Trade Commission maintains an email address for reporting suspected messages (spam@uce.gov). The purpose of that service is to provide consumers with a central place to report deceptive messages and to provide a repository for researchers and law enforcement to understand better and counter the activities.

The problem is bigger than spam, and unfortunately, the responsibility for understanding and protecting ourselves from the potential harm rests squarely on each of our shoulders. For those of us who are responsible for young children or aging relatives, that responsibility has increased enormously. Having email can be an essential connection to the rest of society for someone who is unable to get out much, such as an aging relative. Keeping these at-risk individuals safe from the bad

---

[5] US Postal System Publication 278 - U.S. Postal Inspection Service - A Guide for the U.S. Congress, February 2008, PSN 7610-08-000-4312; available at https://about.usps.com/publications/pub278/welcome.htm

guys can be a time-intensive problem. Understanding the potential and limiting the possibilities for such problems is an important first step to keeping ourselves, and our loved ones, safe.

MALICIOUS ELECTRONIC MESSAGING—WHAT IS IT?

Electronic messaging comprises the entire space of text messages, social media postings, all the way to email. An amazing array of malicious activity is possible over these media. We can separate the malicious activity into two general types. One type is messaging that includes links to malicious software either as attached executable programs or as links to places that malicious software can be downloaded from. Another broad category of malicious electronic messaging is messaging that incites the reader or introduces the reader to actions that are contrary to the reader's best interest. Of these two categories, the second is usually easier to detect than the first.

The category of malicious messaging that incites or induces a reader to actions that are contrary to the reader's best interests include what are called begging emails or phishing emails. Phishing is the art of tricking an individual into responding to a communication crafted for a nefarious purpose. Common mediums used in phishing include email, SMS (texting), phone communication, mail, MMS (chat), and so on. Phishing directly targets the users of systems rather than the systems themselves; however, users may then inadvertently open the door to their systems. Phishing includes messages that ask the reader to participate in some sort of activity to the benefit of the originator of the message. This could be a request for funds for a humanitarian relief operation, a cancer survivor fund, a legal defense fund, or simply a request for support.

Some of these messages are believable and heart rending. This characteristic of appealing to the emotional center of the brain is a key to the attacker's success at getting a reader to do something that he should not. For example, an email or a message may say, "I am stuck in a foreign city and my passport has been stolen! I don't have any money, either. Would you please let me $4000 so I can get back home?" An initial response, if we get to receive this type of message from a close friend or relative, would be to react unthinkingly and to comply with the request for emergency funds. After all, that is what friends do: they help each other. This is a quite common scam, sometimes resulting in multiple people losing the money that they thought they were wiring to help out a friend in need.

Another unfortunate scam that is seen all too often is a request for material support for either medical treatment of extreme types or for some sort of humanitarian relief operation. For example, a distraught mother may request funds to help her child get treatment for a rare disease. Typically, this type of message includes detailed descriptions of what's been tried, what has not worked and the fact that they have had a lot of bad luck, which is why they are simply asking for a very small donation from many, many different people so that a child (typically a very adorable looking child) can be saved.

A variation on this scam is to set up donation request messages for large humanitarian disasters such as hurricanes, tsunamis, or earthquakes. Well-meaning people are duped by these messages: the scam artist winds up siphoning money from the donors. The money will never go to the benefit of the poor people who have suffered the tragedy.

Probably the best known of these scam messages are what is called the Nigerian scam or the Advance Fee scam. It is worth pointing out that not all these emails are from Nigeria: they come from all over the world.[6] In this type of scam, the perpetrator makes contact asking for either what sounds like legitimate business relationship to create a multijurisdictional transactions or perhaps an introduction into a foreign country. A variation on this scam is simply to establish a personal relationship. Sometimes the fraudulent nature of the scam is obvious from the beginning, such as when the sender asks for assistance to sneak a fortune out of his or her home country, promising to pay the recipient a large fee for such assistance. The very obviousness of the fraudulent aspect is most interesting about this. A reason for including this level

---

[6] In fact, this same conceptual scam was known previously as the Spanish Prisoner con. A few sources well worth reading include:

"The long, weird history of the Nigerian e-mail scam" by Finn Brunton, Boston Globe, May 19, 2013. Available online at http://www.bostonglobe.com/ideas/2013/05/18/the-long-weird-history-nigerian-mail-scam/C8bIhwQSVoygYtrlxsJTlJ/story.html

"What I Learned Hanging Out with Nigerian Email Scammers" by Erika Eichelberger, Mother Jones, March 20, 2014, available online at http://www.motherjones.com/politics/2014/03/what-i-learned-from-nigerian-scammers

of detail in the enticement message is simply to cull the recipients and respondents to only those who are likely to fall for the scam based on greed, ignorance, or a combination of the two.[7]

The well-known adage that "if it seems to be good to be true, it probably is" holds true in this case. Being suspicious, even when the offer seems to be genuine, is important. This approach may strike some as being overly paranoid about the nature of human relations, but the history of those who have been conned indicates that a healthy dose of suspicion is indeed warranted.

Suspicion is particularly warranted with a variation that may not appear to be as obvious. In this variant, an electronic message received, sometimes on social media but other times via email, says something to the effect of "I saw your profile online and I would like to get to know you as a friend." Typically, these are aimed at individuals who might be dating online, looking for companionship, or who seem like obvious targets for an "escalation enticement." This type of escalation enticement typically has the perpetrator pretending to want simply to be friends. Once friendship is established, it quickly evolves to a series of escalating requests. The first request may be for some trivial type of assistance, perhaps finding an article of clothing or some other type of good or service. It is hard to say no to something that is easy and which would bring joy to someone else. This good deed opens the door to further requests, perhaps for a very small loan or request for assistance in getting a visa. As the target responds to the enticements, the requests continue to be escalated in both significance and importance. There have been cases where people have spent literally thousands of dollars in what they thought was a legitimate friendship or loan only to discover that they have been scammed.[8] These messaging scams can occur over social media such as Facebook, LinkedIn, or Twitter and can occur over text messaging

---

[7] Dr. Cormac Herley of Microsoft Research has written an excellent analysis of this phenomenon: "Why do Nigerian Scammers Say They Are From Nigeria?", available online at http://research.microsoft.com/pubs/167719/whyfromnigeria.pdf

[8] There are an amazing number of news reports of people reporting that they have fallen victim to these types of scams. An example is described in the story "Spokane Woman Falls Victim to Nigerian Boyfriend Scam" by Jeff Humphrey, KXLY4, Sept 8, 2011. Available online at http://www.kxly.com/news/Spokane-Woman-Falls-Victim-To-Nigerian-Boyfriend-Scam/678090

including random text messages to phone numbers just to see who responds, or can be messages in virtual media as well as email.

Another significant problem in malicious electronic messaging is the type of messaging that includes links to sites that provide downloads of malicious software or embedded material that is malicious in nature. In the first case, the link or the embedded material is usually disguised so that the recipient cannot know at first glance that it is malicious. Attackers can use this tactic not only to gain access to individual accounts, but can also use it to access to entire networks of institutions. Once inside, they establish persistence, or the ability to come and go as they please, and just like that, they have maneuvered past the defenses intended to keep them out. These threats, sometimes referred to as "Advanced Persistent Threats" (APTs), are considered to be some of the most prevalent and dangerous threats to the security of systems and data within the modern organization. TrendMicro, a leading security research firm, estimated in a 2012 report that the vast majority of APT breaches involved a highly targeted email-based attack, leading them to conclude that these types of attacks are a favored tactic for compromising the security of networks.[9]

This is one of the critical problems with recognizing or detecting malicious messaging with the embedded links. In a very real sense, electronic messaging is deceitful simply by design: when you look at an electronic message, it is kind of like looking at the outside of a house or the façade of a building. You think you see structure, and in fact, you have been conditioned by life experience to extrapolate from the visual aspect to the functional structure. When you see the front of a building, you imagine automatically that there is in fact a whole building of similar structure behind the front. It is not until you examine what is underneath the façade that you are able to really appreciate what is the actual structure of the edifice.

In electronic messaging, this is also true by design: the presentation of the message is controlled by the software that contains the commands to select the display font, the display color, embedded images, and other

---

[9] Trend Micro Incorporated Research Paper, "Spear-Phishing Email: Most Favored APT Attack Bait", 2012, available online at http://www.trendmicro.com/cloud-content/us/pdfs/security-intelligence/white-papers/wp-spear-phishing-email-most-favored-apt-attack-bait.pdf

content. The more diverse content that a type of messaging uses leads to a richer messaging environment. Conversely, the richer the messaging media, the more opportunity there is to camouflage malicious content within the rich content. A link to a malicious software download site may be camouflaged as a link to a news article, to a blog, or to what appears to be a legitimate information site. It is actually easy to disguise the true nature of an electronic link by displaying one that appears to be quite innocuous. The problem is compounded with other elements. For example, there are URL abbreviation technologies, such as *bitly* or *tinyurl*, that compress long or ungainly links to something a bit more manageable (or that fit within the character limitations of some messaging services). There are also links that redirect the user to another site, perhaps for ease of use, perhaps to collect use information, or perhaps simply to increase the simplicity of the apparent design. These assistive technologies create a situation where your ability to examine the actual link becomes even more difficult.

In some systems, you can actually examine the underlying raw source data of the unformatted message. Depending upon the platform you are using, you have more or less control over this. This control makes it easier or harder for you to understand or discover the natural relationship of the link that is embedded. For platforms that provide you a great deal of insight into the source the raw source message of an electronic message, you have a great deal of power to understand what the actual embedded data are, where they are coming from, whether the source has been spoofed or not, and other pertinent data. However, if you are operating from a smart phone or some other limited operational capability, your ability to discover the underlying actual data is quite limited indeed. This, obviously, restricts your ability to perform investigations before deciding whether to accept or click on a link. The same problem is true with attachments, which includes not only documents but also images. Attachments such as documents, spreadsheets, or other work-related documents can appear to be innocuous, but may in fact hide the fact that they are executable programs that are designed to launch malicious software on to your system. They can act to compromise your security profile, steal your information, and open some sort of backdoor into your system to allow further activities. Examples of these problems are given in the following chapters.

CHAPTER 2

Types of Malicious Messages

The introduction serves to illustrate the space of the problem. However, to understand what malicious messaging is, and what it is not, it is important to start with a specific definition. The definition offered here is the broadest possible, so that our explorations of the topic can include all possible dangers.

Malicious Message: A message in electronic form, mediated by automated information processing systems, that has been crafted or designed to assist in the achievement of a goal that is, in one or more ways, dangerous to the best interests of the recipient.

In simpler terms, it is an electronic message that can cause you, or the systems you are connected to, harm. There you have it: a short and to the point definition, that makes the point clear: you need to defend yourself against someone who intends to harm you. A tricky follow-on to that definition is figuring out what the potential scope of harm is. Can email harm you physically? Well, not by itself, since an email is nothing but a string of electrons. A properly crafted email may harm your computer, your data, or your network or any network to which you are connected. Additionally, a malicious email may possibly lead you into a situation in which physical harm is a possibility.[1]

Herein lays the danger of malicious email: if simply opening an email can cause problems for you, how can you possibly know which emails are safe to open and which ones are not? Further, how can you know whether an attachment is safe to open or not? It is important to realize that there are no 100% solutions. In this book, we are going

---

[1] There is an important caveat to be added: while strings of electrons sent via message cannot harm you in 2014, they may well be able to harm you in the future, as technologies become even more interconnected with each other and with human support systems, such as medical equipment (pace makers, dialysis machines, insulin pumps, etc.) as well as potentially the human body itself. But that is beyond the scope of this exploration.

to review methods and techniques to give you a fighting chance in the ever escalating war between the senders and the receivers of malicious email.

We have set the stage for developing the skills to identify and combat quickly most malicious emails. Why only "most"? That is part of the problem, and is why education is so important: the attackers are constantly learning and refining their techniques to improve their chances of success. That is why the last chapter in this book covers what to do if one-or-more malicious emails successfully find their target. The target might not be you—it might be a colleague or a loved one, it may be a group you belong to, or it may be the resources and/ or systems of your company. In any event, good preparations include not only preventing problems but also being ready to react should a problem occur.

A word closely associated with malicious messaging is "phishing." This word is pronounced the same as the word "fishing" and it refers to a set of actions done to get victims to reveal sensitive information, such as bank account details, login credentials, passwords, or detailed personal information. In other words, the attacker is fishing for information. Phishing is closely associated with malicious messaging because the easiest way for attackers to execute this type of attack is by the use of messaging technologies, primarily email.

Recognizing that phishing is one of the great threats to an individual or institution, many researchers have set out to find an answer or create a tool that will prevent phishing attacks. Others have studied how the users can be better prepared to defend against such attacks, but nobody has done the research that ties it together into a holistic defense strategy. Some of this work brings together the research and practical knowledge assembled by many other sources, creating a unified framework for defending against phishing attacks. Through the fusion of various studies, a more robust and complete defense strategy can be created, and that through its implementation, individuals and organization will reduce the number of successful phishing attacks experienced annually. Until that work is completed and solutions are deployed, it is up to the individual user to understand and take steps to guard against these types of attacks.

In order to discuss malicious messages, I have divided the types into several categories of features. It is important to point out that these feature types are not exclusive: a malicious message can have several of the type features embedded in one message. However, in order to discuss the problem space, it is easier to separate and consider the problems individually. Once you know what the types of problems are, you are better able to recognize and avoid the problems.

It is important to point out that malicious messaging is not always spam, formally known as Unsolicited Commercial Email (UCE). UCE can clog your inbox, be very annoying, and steal time from more productive activities, but may not be malicious per se. Email and other forms of electronic messaging stray into the malicious zone when the purpose of the message goes beyond the simple advertising of a product. It can be very difficult indeed to differentiate annoying-but-legitimate unsolicited messages from malicious messaging. In fact, malicious email sometimes can even disguise itself as legitimate unsolicited messages in order to trick you into opening the email.[2]

Here are some examples of malicious email:

- invitations to participate in some activity, such as an employment scheme, that can result in theft of money (usually from the recipient);
- requests or demands to click on an embedded link, which results in your unwitting participation in fraudulent activity, such as traffic driving or click fraud, or your unknowing download of unwanted software or material, including viruses or pornographic material;
- requests or demands that attachments to the email be reviewed, where the attachment is malicious software that is executed when opened, embedding software in your computer.

These are but a few of the types of malicious email behavior seen. Rather than cataloging all types, we can generalize certain characteristics that can assist you in making the judgment call: "Is this email legitimate and is it safe to open?"

---

[2] The use of the term UCE rather than "spam" is to avoid the practice of confusing a food product with an interesting history, Spam, with the activities of mass marketers.

FEATURE TYPES OF MALICIOUS MESSAGES

The feature types of malicious messages are all intended to accomplish substantially the same purpose: to get the recipient to do something. The something can be responding to the email, clicking on an embedded link, or opening an attachment. Thus, we can quickly focus in on four primary feature types: appeals to emotion, trickery, subversive links, and subversive attachments. After describing the feature types, I have included real examples of actual emails that illustrate one or more of the feature types.

Appeals to Emotion

Emotion is a powerful motivator for human beings. Research has shown that emotional states can affect physical and mental health and can be responsible for hormonal changes in the body[3]. The sender hopes to get a recipient to act without considering if their emotions are being manipulated. Emotions that are common targets for bad guys to exploit include (but are not limited to) the following:

- emotions associated with comparative success, such as ambition, envy, narcissism, and greed;
- those associated with authority, such as intimidation, obligation, or pride;
- those associated with compassion, such as sympathy or kindness;
- those associated with paranoia, such as anger, bitterness, and fear; and
- those associated with community, such as courage and love.

Trickery

Disguising an electronic message to appear to be legitimate is an appallingly effective way to get recipients to do something they may not normally do. This approach is particularly effective when combined with an appeal to emotion. Often, these electronic messages include precise

---

[3] There are many scientific sources for research supporting this statement. An example is James, et al., "The influence of happiness, anger, and anxiety on the blood pressure of borderline hypertensives." Psychosom Med. 1986; 48(7): 502–508. Abstract available at http://www.ncbi.nlm.nih.gov/pubmed/3763789.

copies of official logos, images, and other symbols of authenticity, such as trademark or copyright logos. The entire design of these types of messages is to convey an overwhelming sense of authenticity to the recipient so that trust will be implied. In addition, when that trust is effectively established through such trickery, the recipient's defenses are reduced, thus increasing the probability that the goal of the sender will be accomplished.

Subversive Links

It is common to receive an electronic message with an embedded link to a website, a document, or some other asset. The problem is that these links are not always what they appear to be. It is possible to disguise a link to hide its true nature. For example, using appearance coding, a link to http://www.exampleofmaliciouslink.com could be disguised to look like something innocuous, like http://www.funwithpuppies.org. This is quite dangerous, as it can be difficult to discover what the actual link in the message is, depending on what platform the recipient is using to read messages. Some platforms, such as fully functioning desktop computers, provide enough functionality that users are able to look behind the curtain to discover the truth. Other platforms, such as some phones, have limited support to users to discover the true content of links. The purpose of subversive links is to get the recipient to load a website that then unleashes the attack on the recipient. Typically, this consists of downloading malicious software automatically. Because of this, a first order recommendation is never to click on a link in an electronic message. Instead, if you really feel like you need to find out what is at the link, use the various tricks at your disposal to discover the actual content. A few of these will be discussed later in the book, but a caveat remains that there are so many platforms, no discussion can possibly be complete and you should take a few minutes to find out how to do this on each of your devices. It is not difficult, as we will see, and can save you a world of pain.

Subversive Attachments

In a similar fashion, it is possible to disguise attachments to look quite legitimate. One common technique is to hide attachment file extensions (such as .doc or .txt) so that the recipient cannot easily detect that the attachment is actually an executable program. Double-clicking on the attachment in the electronic message launches the file via the default application for that file type. Again, the first order recommendation is never to launch an attachment from within an electronic message. If you feel like you need to examine an attachment, you can save it to a protected area in your storage area and then use the directory listing to examine the file naming structure. To examine the contents of the file, you can use the File Open With command on your computer to look at the contents with a text editor, such as a note pad application. If you were expecting it to be a word processing document and all you see is a bunch of symbols or what appear to be hieroglyphs, then you know immediately that the file may not be what you expected it to be. If you are not able to ascertain to a reasonable level of certainty that it is a legitimate file, you should delete it. Alternatively, if you are in an enterprise environment, your network security people might want to examine the file.

A Further Complication

Rarely does the electronic mail have the return address of BadGuy@ badguys.com. Instead, the sender identification will be designed to appear legitimate, innocuous, authoritative, or a combination of all those elements. A favorite trick is to use common names, so that the recipient will assume it is an acquaintance. In these days of social networks, where we have contact lists that number in the thousands, this type of disguise works fairly well to deceive the recipient. Another trick is to use the name of a celebrity or a slight variation on the name of a celebrity. The commonality of the name is such that the defenses of the recipient are reduced simply because the brain is tricked into a sense of normalcy. Electronic messages that are disguised to appear to come from authoritative sources, such as banks or government agencies, naturally have the sender identification modified to appear to be legitimate elements of the source.

All of these elements combine to create what can be an amazing array of tricks to deal with. The knowledge needed is simple, through awareness of the problem, a basic understanding of electronic messaging, and the development of a suspicious approach to electronic messaging. Then simply being cautious can provide an enormous amount of protection against these types of attacks.

EXAMPLES OF MALICIOUS MESSAGES

The following examples are all real; they are copied verbatim from received emails. The message content itself is presented, with an analysis of the types of issues that are easily noted that provide evidence that the message is problematic. Some of the elements are obvious: poor grammar, misspellings, or punctuation mistakes. Other elements are more subtle, until you get used to picking them out in messages. Each of these includes one or more of the feature types discussed earlier.

An Appeal to Emotion

Probably the best known of all malicious emails is the email that invites the recipient to participate in a shady activity with the promise of an enormous payout at the end. There are endless varieties of this type of email: the Nigerian 419 scam, the stranded passenger scam, the lonely-hearts scam, the unlucky inheritor scam, and others. A common version of this type of email is a plea for help combined with an offer to share in good fortune, as noted in the following example:

> My Name is Miss Hanna Gaddafi,I growed up and found that i am an adopted daughter of Late Muammar Gaddafi,former president of Libya who died on October 20, 2011
> I hope you will not find my message offensive since we have not met before and coupled with lots of internet scams going on these days on the internet.
> Due to the critical situation I found myself in Libya, I have managed to sneak into united kingdom as the new government is looking out for all our family members for prosecution or be killed as they killed my father. Am looking for an honest/trusted person to whom i shall hand over deposits my late father deposited on my behalf to be used when am matured enough to handle such enormous treasures (funds including gold and diamonds)if you are the honest/trusted person,kindly get back to me so i can furnish you with the contact information of our family lawyer for the process to kick off immediately as this letter need an urgent attention because the new government is searching for the hidden treasures of my late father therefore treat this as highly confidential and urgent.Waiting to hear from you.
> Miss Hanna Gaddafi

A variation on the scheme exploits religious values to try to get the recipient to respond, as illustrated by the following text of an email (spelling and grammar from original):

From Mother Asetou
My name is Mother Asetou kosta. nationality of Syria's. I am married to late. Mr James kosta. who worked with Ivory Coast embassy in Syria's for nine years before he died in the year October 2009. We were married for twenty years with a two kids. He died after the hilliness that lasted for long last four day. Before his death we were both born again Christians. When my late husband and was alive we deposited the sum of $9.2 Million (Nine Million two thousand Euros) with one of good banks here in Malaysia, presently, this money is still with the bank. Recently my Doctor told me that I would not last for the next three months due to my cancer problem. Though what disturbs me most is my stroke, Having known my condition I decided to donate this fund to church or better still a Christian individual that will utilize this money the way I am going to instruct here in, I want a person or church that will use this fund to churches, orphanages, research canters and widows propagating the word of God and to ensure that the house of God is maintained.
The Bible made us to understand that blessed is the hand that grivet. I took this decision because I have a child that will inherit this money but my son can not carry out this work only because i and my late husband decide to use some of the money to work for God and live some f or our son to have a better live, our son is just 14year old with his elder sister 16 now and been grow up in Africa, he have low mentality and my husband's relatives are not Christians and I don't want my family hard earned money t o be misused by unbelievers. I don't want a situation where this money will be used in an ungodly manner. Hence the reason for taking this bold decision, I am not afraid of death hence I know where I am going to. I know that I am going to be in the bosom of the Lord. Exodus 14 VS 14says that the lord will fight my case and I shall hold my peace. I want your t telephone communication in this regard because of my health because of the presence of my family relatives around me always; I don't want any of my

husband family relatives to receive this money. With God all things are possible.

As soon as I receive your reply I shall give you the contact of the Finance/bank. I will also issue you a letter of authority that will empower you as the new beneficiary of this fund. I want you and the church to always pray for me because the lord is my shepherd. My happiness is that I live a life of a worthy Christian. Whoever that wants to serve the Lord must serve him in spirit and truth. Please always be prayerful all through your life. Any delay in your reply will give me room in sourcing for a church or Christian individual for this same purpose.

Please assure me that you will act accordingly as I stated here.

Remain blessed in the name of the Lord.

Mother Asetou kosta.

What these messages attempt to do is establish contact with a person, who will then be systematically exploited for as much money as the scammers can get.

At first, a trusting person might well be persuaded by the content of these messages. She is merely a poor young girl on the run from people who want to kill her. Of course, the first instinct is to help! A pious elderly woman who simply wants to spread the religion that has given her so much peace? An adherent of the same religion might feel obligated to assist, even blessed to have been the one chosen. It is in these details that the dangers lay but also where the truth can be revealed.

In the first email, the sender claims to have only recently discovered that she is an adopted daughter of Gaddafi. The first question that springs to mind is, "how did the adoption work, if she was abandoned to the point of being ignorant of the fact?" The second question that follows quickly is, "Was she really adopted or not?" If she had truly managed to grow up ignorant of being an adopted daughter of the most powerful person in the country, then why would she be in danger? Furthermore, if she were an abandoned adopted daughter, then how on earth would she have access to all that wealth? Moreover, it is when one starts critically considering the plausibility of the story that it indeed starts to fall apart.

The same is true with the second email, although it is slightly more subtle than the first. In this one, the sender claims to be an older woman with an enormous amount of money that she wants to be used to spread her religion. Taking the message as truth, it is clear that the woman is poorly educated in English and lost her husband approximately 5 years ago (the email was received in 2013). Her husband had worked at the Ivory Coast Embassy in Syria, and she claims to be of Syrian nationality, but later in the email implies that she resides in Malaysia. That is strange. This poor woman says she only has months to live and needs to find a trustworthy person to carry on the good works of the church, which she cannot trust her children to do, since they are in their teens and the son is not very smart. No word on the daughter's intelligence. Moreover, the two children live in Africa someplace, not in Malaysia with her. Therefore, for a strongly religious person of a religion that values family relationships, her family structure is quite strange. Then there is the question of where did she and her husband gets 9.2 million euros? Euros are not the currency of Syria, the Ivory Coast, or Malaysia, so there must have been a currency exchange to convert the money from its original form to euros. It is indeed possible to have a foreign currency account in some banks in Malaysia, but the question lingers—how did two people in Syria manage to open a foreign currency account in Malaysia with that much money?

Both emails are also not addressed to anyone in particular. If you had a large amount of money that you were trying to do something with, would you not research possible assistants to gauge their ability to be of real assistance? Not everyone knows how to manage millions—how does one even keep track of that much money? Furthermore, the second email claims to want the money to be used for religious purposes, but she does not even ask if the recipient shares her religion; much less verify the sanctity of the recipient.

It is in this level of critical analysis that the messages shed any semblance of legitimacy and actually become comical to read. The more you reread the messages, the more ludicrous they become. This then is a critical part of being able to defend yourself against these types of malicious messages: developing the ability to recognize something as illegitimate simply by reading the content. If you read a message over and over again, asking critical questions about each detail, more questions than answers suggest themselves until the scam becomes apparent.

The Invitation

In this type of malicious email, the recipient is invited to participate in some activity. The invitation seems exclusive or very special, and may include a time component, which adds to the incentive for the recipient to act. For example, the following message offering discounted Apple products implores quick action, since the stock is small.

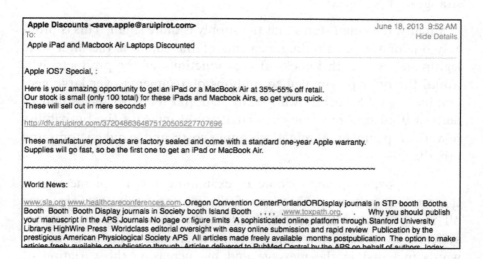

Since Apple products are in great demand and are expensive compared with its alternatives, an unwary recipient might be tempted by this invitation. There are several troubling aspects of this email offer.

First, the date of the email is June 18, 2013 and the lead in sentence of the email is Apple iOS7 Special, with some interesting punctuation. The use of a comma and a colon is different. However, the MacBook Air does not run iOS: that is strictly for the mobile platforms in the Apple family, such as the iPhone and iPad. Further, iOS7 had not yet been released in June, with a scheduled fall 2013 release date. These discrepancies raise serious questions about the validity of this email.

Enticingly, the email offers a very large discount, but the discount is variable from 35% to 55%. So which is it: 35%, 55%, or something in between? The email author(s) might think this range lends credibility to the offer, since it implies that they have legitimately purchased iPads or MacBook Air computers at varying prices, which is why the discount off of retail might vary. A reader might be tempted to interpret the range the same way. But, here is the thing: the legitimate supply chain does not sell these products at varying prices, so this range of discounts just seems strange in this context.

Finally, the email states that the supply is quite small. This is probably one of the most telling elements of the email: if the offer were legitimate, even with knock-off reproductions of the products, why would the offer be emailed to millions of recipients over large geographic areas? Someone who really had 100 iPads to sell would be better off to find local buyers. That would increase the probability of verified payment, eliminate shipping costs, and avoid customs and other tariffs.

An important point to note in examining this email message is the random text at the bottom of the message: this text, scrapped off news feeds, is designed to confuse the spam-detection software systems. By greatly increasing the number and complexity of the words included in the message and by increasing the variation of the content, automated detection of spam is reduced in accuracy. However, a quick visual inspection of the email reveals the random text and alerts the recipient to this trick, which would not be needed for a valid email. Interestingly, sometimes the random text can be placed well below the actual text of the message to reduce the chance that the person receiving the email will actually see the text.

A variation on the Invitation Message is to urge the recipient to take his or her place of recognition in exclusive societies. For example, the following invitation message combines an appeal to vanity with a warning about it being a final notice:

Final Notice <alimentationhewing@refi-isnow.us>

To:

Your Exclusive Invite to be apart of a growing community

June 27, 2013 4:45 AM

Hide Details

This will be your final notice. If you cannot see the message below Click Here

</p>

    This is the final notice regarding your inclusion within the 2013/2014 Edition of Who's Who Among Professionals. We have sent you several emails requesting your inclusion, and so far we have not received any confirmation on your biographical proof.

Most individuals look at the Who's Who as the world's premier source for networking. Our professional network of trusted contacts gives you an advantage in your career, and is one of your most valuable assets. The Who's Who exists to help you make better use of your professional network and help the people you trust in return. Our mission is to connect the world's professionals to make them more productive and successful. We believe that in a globally connected economy, your success as a professional and your competitiveness as a company depends upon faster access to insights and resources that you can trust.

We urge you to Go Here and fill out the appropriate information in order to get the biographical process started. There is no cost or obligation to be listed.

Best of luck in all of your future endeavors,

Be 100% Up to Date in your Industry Get noticed today be happy you did it tomorrow !

alimentation hewing

Managing Directo r

Who's Who Among
119 Chambers Str eet
15th Floor
New York, NY 100 07

To unsub scribe click here:

This message is probably the most unprofessional looking email one could ever imagine, particularly for one that claims to be from a prestigious source of professional individuals. There are odd spaces in words, the name of the "Managing Director" is not capitalized, and the formatting is simply ugly. The return address of "refi-isnow.us" is suspect as well, since it bears little resemblance to a publishing company. But it uses words that can entice the unwary: "exclusive," "final notice," and "premier source." Further, it includes a presumably prestigious New York City address, on the 15th floor as well, leading those not familiar with New York City to potentially be impressed. Those who take the time to look up the address discover that it is six story building, making the 15th floor an extravagant detail indeed.

It is clearly a scam—and a quick search on the internet confirms that status—but the interesting inclusion of links makes it dangerous. The first "Click Here" in light blue is a hot link: it is a clickable link that, if selected, would take you to a website. You cannot tell simply by looking at the "Click Here" words where the link might take you, and therein lies the danger. Then, there is the entire (run-on) sentence in light blue: "Be 100% Up to Date in your Industry Get noticed today be happy you did it tomorrow !," which is also enabled as a hot link. Again, you have no way by simply looking at it to see where it would take you. And finally, there is the hot link after the words "To unsubscribe," helpfully labeled "click here:" Again you have no way of knowing where that link would take you. The range of options is endless: it could take you to a terrorist recruitment site, a site that would launch malicious software (such as viruses) into your computer, or other equally inappropriate places. Later in the book, we will go into how to see what the actual link is, but for now, you just need to know that you should not click on any link you do not understand completely.

The Offer of Money

In this type of malicious email, the recipient is directly offered money. Typically, the details are very sparse, as in the example shown below, but the offer sounds sincere and urges the recipient to act quickly in order to take advantage of the offer.

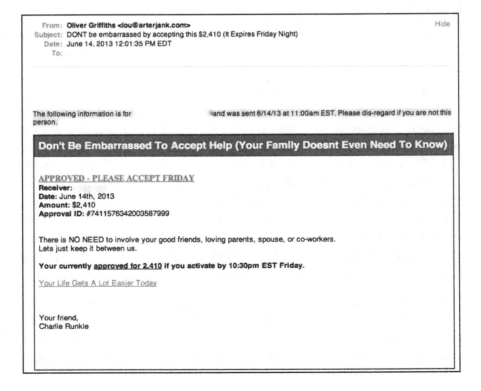

The first element in this email that draws our attention is the subject line, which contains several interesting features. The subject line reads: "Don't be embarrassed by accepting this $2,410 (It Expires Friday Night)." There are three action elements in this subject: emotion, a lure or attraction, and time.

The emotional element is evoked by the use of the phrase, "Don't be embarrassed." A gut level reaction from a normal person would be indignation, followed closely by a desire to prove the implication wrong. This is the same emotional response that is triggered in adolescents when they dare each other to do something. The use of the word "embarrass" casts an aspersion on the reader, implying that the reader is so insecure that he or she might be embarrassed at their state of being or worth. Without thinking, an immediate response is to react in order to counter that implication, to prove that the recipient is not at all embarrassed. This emotional aspect is powerful enough that one sees it often in malicious emails.

There is also an element of conspiracy: no one else needs to know, it can be a secret. This enticement is followed by the promise that the recipient is already approved, with an officious looking approval id, and an underscored point that it will make the recipient's life a lot easier, almost immediately.

The lure or attraction in this case is the money. It is not a huge amount but it is not trivial either. It is enough to get the recipient's attention. The wording is obscure as well: the use of the phrasing "accepting this $2,410" sounds like the money might be offered by a wealthy donor or grant agency. There is no implication that this might be a loan or other type of credit—it just sounds like someone is offering to give away $2,410. And who would turn away from free money? Money is very useful in this life and the average person can find a lot of ways to spend an extra two thousand dollars.

The time component is a deadline that reinforces the emotional impact of the message. The deadline screams at the person to act fast before the good luck evaporates. The day that this message was received was, not coincidentally, Friday. The pressure created by this deadline increases the emotional imperative to act on the message.[4]

All of these elements are duplicated and reinforced by the content of the email. The emotional aspect is reinforced by the parenthetical comment "Your Family Doesnt Even Need To Know." This also speaks directly to those who might be working themselves to death to keep their family in food and clothing: a chance for a windfall would be very attractive. The official looking structure of the email reinforces the lure in two places while adding some impressive details, such as the Approval ID, an impressive looking 19 digit number. The time component is reinforced several times as well, most notably in the capitalized, red lettered, underlined exhortation: "APPROVED - PLEASE ACCEPT FRIDAY."

Clues that this email might not be entirely legitimate also abound. For example, the name and email address in the From line do not match. One might wonder how an "Oliver Griffiths" came to have an email address of "Lou." Then there is the name of the person who signed the email, "Charlie Runkle." Three different names in this email are definitely questionable.

Another clue is in the numerous grammatical oddities. These include a hyphen in the word disregard, even though one is not needed, the lack of an apostrophe in the words "doesn't" and "let's," the misspelling of the word "you're" as "your," and the use in closing of "Your Friend."

And, finally, there is the question about the terms: is this a loan, a grant, free money, or what? Would the recipient be required to do work for the money? All these things are left unclear, a point which an unwary reader may not even notice.

The Alert

In The Alert, a recipient is warned that her account has been compromised and needs to immediately change their passwords and possibly other login credentials to keep their account information safe. An

---

[4] For those who would like to understand the psychology better, Frank Stajano and Paul Wilson have a very readable exploration titled "Understanding Scam Victims: Seven Principles for System Security" which was published in Communications of the ACM in March 2011 (vol. 54, no. 3), available online at http://www.cl.cam.ac.uk/~fms27/papers/2011-StajanoWil-scam.pdf.

example is shown below, purportedly from Capital One. It looks very authentic, even using official Capital One logos. And it is very scary indeed, with the subject line of "Account Locked Notification" guaranteed to spike a recipient's blood pressure. Close analysis, however, reveals it to be an entire fraud.

This example is much more carefully constructed than the previous examples. The use of the official logos, the structure of the email, the inclusion of the Log In button—all of these design elements come together to reassure the recipient that the email is legitimate. Thus, it takes a little extra effort to determine whether it is legitimate or not.

Let us start with the concept of the email. I do not have a Capital One account, so why would Capital One be sending me an email warning me about "unusual activity" in my account? It would be unusual to have any activity at all, considering that there is no account. Unless there was a problem with identity theft, which is a very real issue, there should be no account. Assuming we can rule out identity theft, the very concept of the email is a clue that it is not legitimate.

Moving on to the From line: it looks legitimate on its face, with the sender being identified as capitalone@email.capitalone.com. Just because it looks legitimate does not mean it is. Looking into the internals of the email, it turns out that the real From email address is from cafe24.com, which is a Chinese language website (how to actually do this will be covered later in the book). This discovery reinforces the most important element of detecting and combatting malicious email: do not believe what you see at first glance. Always dig deeper to find out what the truth of the matter is.

The email itself contains only a few suspect features. The links in the upper right hand corner lend an air of authenticity to the email, as does the body structure. However, there are some clues that all is not as it might seem. The use of the ® symbol in the subject line at the end of the "Account Locked Notification" is strange—why should a symbol that means something is registered, such as a trademark or slogan, be used next to a generic notification? This same strange use of official looking notation continues in the email body, with SM symbol appended to Capital One Online. While Capital One does indeed offer online banking, much like most other banks today, their Service Marked offering is called Capital One 360, not Capital One Online. This is fairly esoteric knowledge that not everyone would have, but it is still worth keeping in mind.

The body of the message is not poorly constructed. There is really only one grammatical error that leaps out, but it is associated with a word that would be highly unusual to be included in this type of message, if it is to be legitimate. That is the word "kindly," which in this email is not capitalized even though it begins a sentence. Also, the use of "kindly" in this context is not normal usage and just seems off. If this was a legitimate email, it should not be necessary to beg with someone to kindly perform an action, particularly if online access to their funds had been suspended.

The sentence then concludes with, "so we can complete your security update." This sentence is contextually different. The email first states that access to the account has been suspended due to unusual activity, but then changes to a security update process. These are two completely different processes and combining them in one very short email really raises suspicions. But it is a clever construction: by first raising the fear level of the recipient and then by offering a quick fix, the probability that a recipient will actually click on the link to "fix the security" increases.

The use of links embedded in the email seems like something a reasonable sender would do, and in fact, legitimate emails include them all the time. They are dangerous though, simply because what you see in a formatted message is only and exactly what the sender wants you to see. In this case, the sender has configured the presentation of the link to make it look like it goes to www.capitalone.com, which in fact is the legitimate website for Capital One, although they prefer users to go to the https version, which has encryption services enabled to protect the communications. Looking inside the email, we discover that the link does not in fact go to Capital One, but directs the person who clicks on the link to the website adinship.ch.

The term "phishing," which is pronounced "fishing" (as in with a rod and bait), was introduced earlier. This email is a prime example of a phishing email: it is intended to lure the catch, which is the recipient, with the bait, which is the fear of losing money, to bite the hook, which is clicking on the link that will prompt the recipient to enter in all kinds of personal information, which will then allow the malicious sender to indeed compromise the recipient's bank accounts.

Another example of a phishing email is the one pictured below. This variation is also very common. In this variant, the scare tactic is loss of email access and the bait is the ability to restore full access immediately by clicking on the link.

From: **The George Washington University <wahlbeck@gwu.edu>**
Subject: Mail protection service Webmail Log
Date: June 20, 2013 2:08:20 PM EDT
To:

Welcome to The George Washington University

Mail protection service Webmail Log

Mail protection service has detected some suspicious Alert on your
online your Webmail and has been temporarily restricted because your
account has been suspended.

Restore & Protect Account Now.

© 2013, The George Washington University

Again, this email looks at first glance like it might be authentic. That
is a key to its success as a way to gather personal information from actual users. Effective organizations continually remind customers and users
that these types of communications are never authentic and that users
should never either believe the email or respond, either by replying or
clicking on the link.

A particularly problematic version of this type of malicious message is illustrated by the following email that purports to be from Wells
Fargo, another well-known financial institution.

This email does not include all the graphics and professional layout
of the fraudulent Capital One email, but still it manages to look official
enough, with a plausible return address, signature block, and lots of
legal disclaimers. The danger here lies in the attachment. The text of the
message is quite simple and direct: it asks the recipient, nicely, to "check
the attached documents."

This request is tempting from at least two perspectives. If the recipient is indeed a customer of Wells Fargo, the recipient may be tempted to
open the attachment to see what information is being sent. On the other
hand, if the recipient is not a customer, then the recipient may think that

the information has been sent to the wrong email address by mistake. In that case, the recipient may be tempted to open the attachment out of curiosity, to see what the intended recipient's financial situation might be, or altruistically, in an attempt to determine the correct end address for the material.

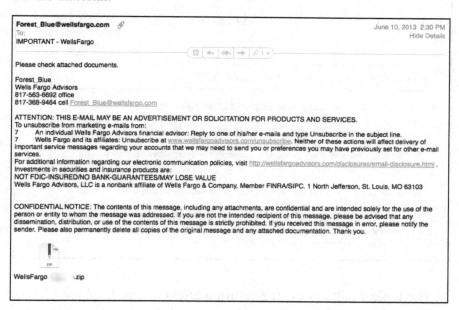

Opening the attachment is a very, very bad idea. In this particular case, the attachment contains malicious software which, when unzipped, would execute to install on the recipient's computer. The use of a zipped file is particularly clever, as the compression assists in bypassing some protection software. In this instance, it was easy to see, simply by examination, that the file was a zipped file. This alone was enough to raise suspicions regarding the content of the actual attachment. In some instances of malicious attachments, it can be very difficult to identify the actual file type of the attachment. We will cover how to examine attachment types safely later in the book.

The Inside Scoop

In this type of malicious email, the sender offers to share special or secret information with the recipient that will help with health issues, financial issues, or other common problems. An example of this type of email is shown below, which offers to share with you a secret cure for high blood pressure and high cholesterol that the medical establishment does not want you to know about.

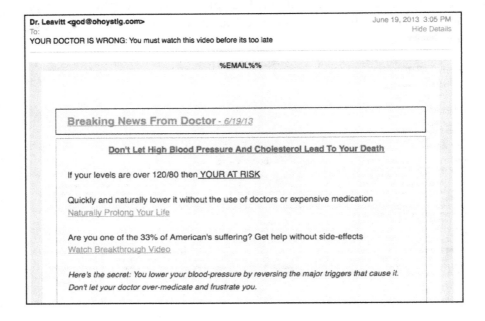

The typical telltales exist: a return address of "god," abuse of bold and capitalization, fear tactics, and the appeal of hidden knowledge that the establishment does not want you to know. Many of these emails do not provide details: you have to click through to get the secret. And once they have your email, they can then make money selling it to other email marketers. Of course, they can also entice you to purchase alternative medicines, some of which are extremely dangerous. Some of the remedies being sold may even seem healthy and safe, since they are herbs. What some potential customers do not realize is that not all herbs are safe and that some herbs are only safe in certain circumstances. For example, a herb called yohimbe[5] actually causes high blood pressure, so taking it would make a problem with hypertension worse, not better.

---

[5] As noted by the American Cancer Society, "yohimbe is an evergreen tree native to western Africa. ... Yohimbe bark has been declared an unsafe herb in Germany because of such complications as increased heart rate and blood pressure, and even kidney failure." http://www.cancer.org/treatment/treatmentsandsideeffects/complementaryandalternativemedicine/herbsvitaminsandminerals/yohimbe.

The Masked Email

Certain emails look legitimate because they seem to come from well-known sources. The email shown below claims to be from Match.com, a well-known online dating site. It is not however. It is fake, pretending to be from Match.com, trying to get you to click on the embedded links. The entirety of the email is shown: the only thing there is the link. But again, you do not know just by looking what is behind the link.

Match.com <reply@guildtrade.co.uk>	June 3, 2013 11:25 AM
To:	Hide Details
See Who's on Match.com **- It's Free to Look!**	

See Who's on Match.com - It's Free to Look!

The Big Lie

Chain emails sent and resent amongst people who know and trust each other can promulgate falsehoods into effects of staggering proportion. Typically, these emails take some situation, recast it in an overtly political tone, and play to the emotional sympathies associated with patriotism, religion, or family love. The email shown below is an example of a blatant falsehood being promulgated with a great deal of plausibility through trusted networks of friends and relatives. The interesting thing about this is the nature of the falsehood: the email blames the "socialist government" for a business decision that may (or may not) have occurred: the details are disputed.[6] Independent of the veracity of the actual cancellation of the account, and the reasons for that if it indeed occurred, which is really none of our business, Bank of America is not a government organization, much less a socialist government organization. The entire purpose of this message can be interpreted as a subtle attack upon support for the government at the very real expense of Bank of America. It received enough publicity that the National Rifle

---

[6] For an interesting set of discussions on this particular email, see the following URLs:
http://www.dailykos.com/story/2012/10/22/1148424/-They-don-t-even-know-WTF-it-means#
http://www.snopes.com/politics/guns/bankofamerica.asp
http://www.nraila.org/news-issues/articles/2012/nra-investigating-story-concerning-bank-of-america.aspx?s&st&ps

Association investigated the story, including a statement from the Bank that it does "not have a policy that would deny banking services to entities because they are in the firearms industry. Bank of America has banking relationships with retailers, manufacturers and other related companies."[7] A search for similar stories on Google revealed "about 6300 results," many of them with exactly the same language. The story reached an astonishing number of people, simply through the mechanism of sharing.

September 25, 2012 12:48 AM
Hide Details

To: Undisclosed-Recipient:;
Fw: Bank of America - : McMillan Mfg in Phoenix, Arizona

----- Original Message -----
From:
To: undisclosed-recipients:
Sent: Monday, September 24, 2012 7:36 PM
Subject: Fwd: Bank of America - : McMillan Mfg in Phoenix, Arizona

From the owners of McMillan Mfg in Phoenix, Arizona,
If you do business with Bank of America, you might want to change. They also need to think about changing their name. There is no place in it for America

Second Amendment
This is happening all around us and we are allowing this socialist government to keep growing.

McMillan Mfg in Phoenix, Arizona, was contacted by Bank of America and informed that they will no longer be allowed to use their services (Bank of America)
because they are in the firearms business and support the second amendment.

I am fine with you re-posting it. . . . . Thanks for your support.

Kelly D. McMillan
Director of Operations
McMillan Group International, LLC
623-582-9635
1638 W Knudsen Dr
Phoenix, Arizona 85027
McMillan Integrity-Global Vision
http://www.mcmillanusa.com/
Become a fan of McMillan on Facebook
http://www.facebook.com/McMillanGroupInternational

McMillan Fiberglass Stocks, McMillan Firearms Manufacturing, McMillan Group International have been collectively banking with Bank of America for 12 years.

Today Mr. Ray Fox, Senior Vice President, Market Manager, Business Banking, Global Commercial Banking (Bank of America) came to my office.

He scheduled the meeting as an "account analysis" meeting in order to evaluate the two lines of credit we have with them.
He spent 5 minutes talking about how McMillan has changed in the last 5 years and have become more of a firearms manufacturer than a supplier of accessories.

At this point I interrupted him and asked "Can I possibly save you some time so that you don't waste your breath? What you are going to tell me is that because we are in the firearms manufacturing business you no longer want my business."

"That is correct", he says.

---

[7] NRA Institute for Legislative Affairs, "NRA Investigating Story Concerning Bank of America," April 27, 2012. Posted at http://www.nraila.org/news-issues/articles/2012/nra-investigating-story-concerning-bank-of-america.aspx?s&st&ps.

The Little Lie

Chain mails can also promulgate information that, while not nearly as malicious, can cause harm or at least potential for harm. The following email is an example of this type of nonsense.

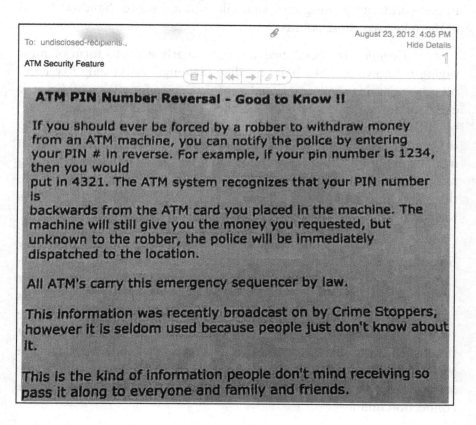

To: undisclosed-recipients.,

August 23, 2012 4:05 PM
Hide Details

ATM Security Feature

ATM PIN Number Reversal - Good to Know !!

If you should ever be forced by a robber to withdraw money from an ATM machine, you can notify the police by entering your PIN # in reverse. For example, if your pin number is 1234, then you would
put in 4321. The ATM system recognizes that your PIN number is
backwards from the ATM card you placed in the machine. The machine will still give you the money you requested, but unknown to the robber, the police will be immediately dispatched to the location.

All ATM's carry this emergency sequencer by law.

This information was recently broadcast on by Crime Stoppers, however it is seldom used because people just don't know about it.

This is the kind of information people don't mind receiving so pass it along to everyone and family and friends.

This email passes along information purporting to be truth, but which in fact false. So what is the danger? Imagine being at an ATM and being held at gunpoint. How easy is it to remember your real PIN? Now imagine entering it in reverse. For many people, entering a PIN is a matter of muscle memory—you do not actually think about the numbers, but enter the PIN through memory of placement of numbers on the pad: top left, top right, middle middle, and bottom left for a PIN of 1359. Trying to enter that in reverse, particularly under pressure, would cause a normal person to have to pause and figure it out slowly, which would provide a clue to the robber that there was something amiss. Furthermore, if the robber was actually aware that no ATM in the United States currently employs this technology, then all the robber would have to do is watch the laboriously entered PIN fail and reverse it for a successful next attempt. Sure, in the scheme of things, this is probably not the worst thing in the world, but passing such small lies around wastes bandwidth and at the very least cause confusion.

Like Farming: In social media, a particularly noxious form of messaging is known as "like bait" or "like farming." A typical "like bait" message contains some emotional appeal, such as for a lost child, a sick child, or some innocuous message such as "share if you hate cancer" or "I bet you won't share this." These messages are blatant attempts to drive up the number of people that are reached by certain pages. Social media companies, such as Facebook, counter these tactics with filtering technologies, but it is certain that with money from advertising at risk, the people engaging in these types of tactics will simply find new ways to spam.

Some of these like-farming efforts are potentially dangerous, simply because they abuse real images of people without consent, thereby exposing those people to potential harm. A particularly appalling example of this was the theft of a photo of a young girl named Katie, who was repackaged as "Mallory." The post showed the photo along with the request: "This is my sister Mallory. She has Down syndrome and doesn't think she's beautiful. Please like this photo so I can show her later that she truly is beautiful." The family discovered this abuse when people started emailing them about their daughter, after having discovered the connection online.[8]

---

[8] This story was covered in many outlets; one instance is "Social Media Stole My Daughter's Identity," published Oct 26, 2012, at http://www.news.com.au/technology/facebook-stole-my-disabled-daughters-identity/story-e6frfrnr-1226503776416.

CHAPTER 3

Thinking Like the Enemy

Understanding the psychology of a phishing attack can be as much of a resource to stopping it as any technology or security analysis. Understanding both sides of the attack gives the defender a better perspective as to what makes his/her organization vulnerable, and just how far the attacker might go to exploit that vulnerability. For example, understanding that the motivating factor of one class of attacker might solely be glory driven would imply that their resolve to work through layers of defense could be minimal, leading them to give up quickly in order to find an easier target. However, that same class of attacker might be more determined if the target was to be perceived as having high value, since compromising a higher value target would yield greater prestige and greater validation. For senders of malicious email, this duality is particularly true: the vast majority of attacks are aimed at anyone who will respond while a small minority of attacks are exquisitely targeted for very high value targets.

There are two primary goals for a sender of a malicious email. The first goal is for you to actually see the email. This means that the email needs to be constructed to avoid automated scanning and quarantining programs. The second goal is to have you act on the email. In some cases, this is as simple as opening it and reading it. In other cases, the sender wants you to open an attachment.

And therein lies a significant challenge: how to understand the goals and intentions of the sender of malicious email. For you to actually see the email, it must reach you, which means it must be targeted, it must have addressing that you do not recognize as malicious, and it must have content that passes through any filters that might be on your system. In order for you to actually act on the message—be that clicking, opening attachments, sharing, or replying, the seen message must be appropriate to your needs, wants, and likes (or dislikes).

Targeting: Malicious email may be targeted specifically at you or may be shotgunned to as many recipients as possible. The email that is sent to a wide range of recipients is generally more easily identifiable as potentially malicious. The email that specifically targets you can be extremely difficult to detect. There is a cost trade-off to the sender: it is cheap and easy to send the same email to thousands of recipients, while it is quite costly to develop the knowledge base required to specifically target a single person in a believable manner. The two types of email are referred to as UnTargeted Malicious Email (UTME) and Targeted Malicious Email (TME). UTME is sent to as many people as possible: it is, by definition, un-targeted. TME, also known as spear-phishing (a play on the term "spear-fishing") is much more precise, targeting as few as one individual with a highly personalized attack designed to be as effective as possible. It is very expensive to develop the level of information about a single person—their work habits, their conversations, their likes and dislikes, and son on—to mount an effective TME attack, so that level of effort is typically reserved only for very high value targets. An example of the type of target that would warrant this type of effort would be someone in a high technology enterprise who has easy access to the details of marketing plans or development ideas. Getting such a person to open an attachment in an email can open the entire corporation's network to the attackers, allowing them unfettered access to very sensitive data.

Addressing: Malicious email senders normally do not want their real identities to be discovered, so may use a variety of hiding techniques to mask the true source of the email. The visible sender identity may be forged as that of a very common name, to mimic an identity in your contacts list, or as that of a celebrity. One of the first tricks to identify potential malicious email is to look at the invisible parts of the addressing to see what it really looks like. Chapter 4 will deal with this in detail.

Content: Malicious email can contain a variety of content types that are dangerous. Some of the most innocuous malicious messaging is chain messages, typically forwarded or shared many times, which contains a distorted version of events designed to elicit an emotional response in the recipient. The purpose of these malicious emails is to affect belief structures, and these mails are called either Meme-Propaganda or Memetic Attacks. The examples provided in Chapter 2 covered a large variety of the types of content in malicious messages, although it is worth noting that the imaginations of the attackers are without bounds. In fact, they are quite amazing. One example of a malicious message alerted a recipient to a purported dead body found outside and asked that the recipient open the attachment to identify the decedent. This simply illustrates that nothing at all is off-limits.

The people who generate malicious messages, be it for theft of personal information, solicitation of relationships, like-farming, or any of the other motivations, have one and only one thing in common: they are people. Beyond that, they vary in amazing number of ways. Some are very poor, operating out of internet cafes under the watch of gang leaders. Some are modestly well-off, operating out of their homes or a local cafe. Others are wealthy, having been in the game for long enough to reap a lot of rewards. Two stories of real people help to illustrate who these people are.

Adam Vitale: Mr. Vitale pleaded guilty in 2008 to violating US Federal law for spamming people. He claimed to be making $40,000 per week doing this. He specialized in stock price scams, so that the insiders could profit from selling stocks whose prices had artificially inflated as a result of their activities, although was willing to engage in a variety of other scams, including advertising computer security software.[1]

Two Nigerian Scammers: Mother Jones reporter Erika Eichelberger wrote of meeting two young men engaged in what they referred to as trickery, "insist[ing] that tricking someone is not the same thing

---

[1] Various sources that covered Adam Vitale include:
Reuters, "NY Man Pleads Guiltly to Spamming AOL Subscribers", Jun 11, 2007, http://www.reuters.com/article/2007/06/11/us-crime-spam-idUSN1120537620070611.
Tynan, Dan. "Will the Real Spam King Please Stand Up?", published in PC World, Oct 16, 2008; republished in the Washington Post, available at http://www.washingtonpost.com/wp-dyn/content/article/2008/10/13/AR2008101302311.html.
US Attorney, Southern District of New York, "Brooklyn Man Pleads Guilty in Participating in Massive AOL Spam Scheme." June 11, 2007, http://www.justice.gov/usao/nys/pressreleases/June07/vitalepleapr.pdf.

as stealing" from them. These two men participate in advance-fee scams, also known at the 419 scam, and claim to be worth about $60,000 each.[2]

These two stories illustrate the great variety, and it is important to underscore that a malicious email message may be from someone trying to steal your money, your time, or your information. Because of the wide range of motivations, it is impossible to specify a single type of person who engages in this activity. Instead, it is all types of persons, from all over the world, who have varying moral bases.

The motivation is clear: it is to gain something that they would not otherwise have. In some cases, the motivation is to get you to send money directly. In other cases, it is to get you to click on a link that will download malicious software onto your computer. In yet other cases, the motivation is to get you to open an attachment that will enable activity on your computer that you would rather not have happening.

The motivation could be to harness the power of your computer as a zombie member of a botnet, which can then be rented out by the hour for a variety of activities, including conducting denial of service attacks on specific systems. Or the motivation might be to install software on your computer that allows the controlling person access to all of your data, including sensitive company data. A very common motivation is simply to get you to enter sensitive personal information into a reply email or a website so that the person can then steal your identity, empty your bank account, or use your electronic identity for nefarious purposes.

The motivations range from simple, such as the meter repair scam detected in Oregon, to viciously clever, such as a Netflix user phishing scam. In the meter repair scam, customers were contacted with demands for hundreds of dollars for repairs to their meters, with the threat that if they did not pay, their electrical service would be turned off.[3] In the Netflix user phishing scam, users are duped into going to a website that looks

---

[2] Eichelberger, Erika. "What I Learned Hanging Out With Nigerian Email Scammers", Mar 20, 2014. Available at http://www.motherjones.com/politics/2014/03/what-i-learned-from-nigerian-scammers.

[3] "PUD Warns Customers About Meter Repair Scam", April 30, 2014. Available at http://www.thechronicleonline.com/news/article_44926c5e-d07b-11e3-ad80-001a4bc f887a.html.

like the real Netflix site but which is not. The trick is enabled through the purchase of sponsored ads, pop-up windows, or emails. When the phony website loads, it directs the user to access Member Services and provides a toll-free number for the member to call. The person at the end of that toll-free number is not a Netflix employee at all, but in fact a scammer. The phone person then walks the customer through a software download process that provides the scammers with backdoor access to the customer's computer.[4]

Unfortunately, this range of motivations means that focusing on motivation as a way to understand people who are behind malicious messaging is a losing cause. The simple definition of the motivation is theft, but the variety of means through which that theft is accomplished is amazingly large.

Because people in general do not much care to have their money, their identities, or their data stolen, there is a concerted effort by service providers and law enforcement to limit the activities of malicious messagers. Unfortunately, it is a game of steps. When one method or channel is countered, a new method emerges. The bad guys actually study the activities of the defenders and develop methods that are not detectable by their current approaches. What this means is that you must constantly be on guard, waiting for that next surprise.

Success for the bad guys comes when someone opens and replies to their messages, shares a like-farming post, clicks on a malicious link, or opens an attachment. That is the first step in getting access to what they really want, but it is a critical first step and the ultimate success can not occur until that happens.

So, bottom line: do not click on links, do not open attachments, and treat every message with suspicion. But if you feel the need to follow a link or open an attachment, do it carefully.

---

[4] Taylor wrote two stories on this problem:
"Phishing Scam Targeting Netflix May Trick You With Phony Customer Service Reps", Mar 3, 2014. http://www.huffingtonpost.com/2014/03/03/netflix-phishing-scam-customer-support_n_4892048.html.
"Scammers Are Targeting Netflix Users Again, Preying On The Most Trusting Among Us", Apr 17, 2014. http://www.huffingtonpost.com/2014/04/17/netflix-comcast-phishing-_n_5161680.html.

CHAPTER 4

Inside Messaging: Making the Hidden Visible

It is easy to look at an email and not see what is hidden behind the display. In fact, most people would not even suspect that behind a very simple looking email might be lurking some complicated programming. It is both a reality and a shame that bad guys figured out how to trick people into doing things they ordinarily would not do by simply disguising the actions, but with just a little bit of knowledge, you can understand how it works. Through that understanding, you can be more alert as to the potential problems.

EMAIL BASICS

The actual structure of an email consists of several elements. First, there is the header information. This is the electronic equivalent of all the information on the outside of an envelope, plus a bit more. Then there is the body of the message. This is the functional equivalent of a letter inside the envelope. And then there are possible attachments, which can come in many different forms. Each of these three elements is important to understand. The following figure illustrates the standard format of an email.

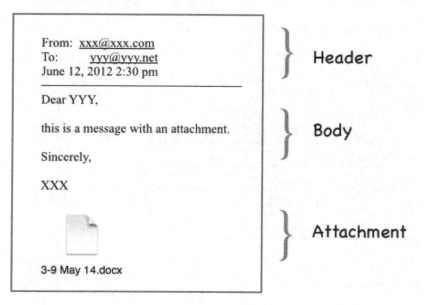

THE HEADER

The header of an email contains a treasure trove of information. In a typical email client, like on a smart phone, in a web browser, or in an email client, the user will not see all of the data that are available. What the user will see is basic information, such as the name of the sender, the names of the "To" recipients, and the names of the "CC" recipients, plus a subject line and the date and time of the message. The hidden details are long and laborious, and not really very useful information for the vast majority of legitimate emails. But for malicious emails, the hidden data contain very useful information indeed. The two figures below show comparisons of the same email: first, the standard display for emails on a smart phone, a web browser, and in an email client; and then the actual information behind that display. This email purports to be from Capital One, the large financial institution. Looking at the header information gives us clues as to whom the message is actually from.

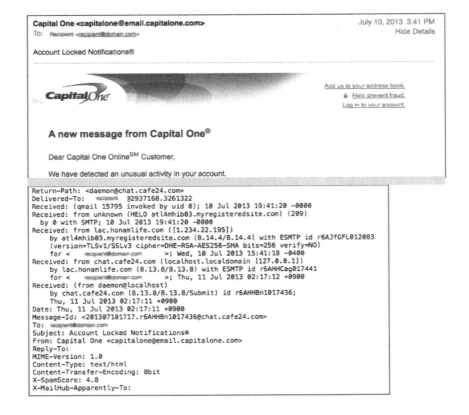

The obvious information that is of interest is the "From" line. But notice that there are many different "From" lines! Which one to pay attention to? A general rule of thumb is to start at the bottom of the header information and work your way up. Let us go through the header information, from the bottom up, focusing on the ones that contain information of use to you. Not all the data included are of particular interest to the normal user, which is why most of them are hidden.

First, look at the second line from the bottom: "X-SpamScore: 4.8." This is a calculated measure of how closely the message matches the parameters most often found in spam messages. In this case, the score of 4.8 is borderline, although the thresholds are configurable. A rule of thumb is that a score above 5 is probably spam, whereas a score below 5 probably is not. But with all the tricks that spammers use to confuse the calculations, such as including a lot of random text hidden behind the presented email, these scores can be manipulated.

Moving up from there, it is very interesting to note that the "Reply-To:' line is blank. The "Reply-To" field is normally filled in with the email address for replying to the message. If you receive an email address with the "Reply-To' field blank and you click the "Reply" button, your email client will generate an email with a blank "To' field. This is not only a clue that something is amiss with the email, but it is also a forcing function to cause a recipient to either fill in the email address or click on one of the embedded links. If the recipient choses to fill in an email address, the address that is obvious in the formatted email is "capitalone@email.capitalone.com'," which is not a legitimate email address: use of this address would result in a message stating that the email cannot be delivered. Thus, the only option left available to the recipient would be to click on one of the links, which is what the sender wants the recipient to do. More about the links in the message body discussion.

Moving up from the "Reply-To' field is the "From" field, which in this case is filled in with the fraudulent email address, "Capital One <capitalone@email.capitalone.com>." This field is very easy to spoof. All the sender has to do is change the settings in the email client and write in what should be seen in that field. As such, it is not a reliable source for sender identification.

Skipping over the "Subject" and "To" fields, since they are obvious in content, we start to get to useful information. In this case, the next line up with the "Message-ID" field. In this example, this field shows a content string of "<201307101717.r6AHHBn1017436@chat.cafe24.com>" and provides a very nice clue as to the actual origin of this message. Looking at the content, we see that there are three parts to the "Message ID": a numerical string (201307101717), a mixed alphanumeric string (r6AHHBn1017436), and a domain identification (chat.cafe24.com).

Message identifiers are supposed to be unique identifiers, so a common technique is to use the date and time of the message generation as the source of the first part.[1] And in comparing the date and time of the message to the first numerical string, we see that there are similarities. The date of the message is given as July 11, 2013, at 2:17 A.M. in the time zone of +9 hours off of Universal Coordinated Time (UTC) (that is what the +0900 means). Looking up an area of the world that is located in that time zone gives a very short set of areas: "East Timor, Indonesia (Sumatra, Java, West & Central Kalimantan only), Japan, Korea (North) (Peoples Democratic Republic of Korea), Korea (South) (Republic of Korea), Palau."[2] The local time in that time zone would have been 9 hours ahead of UTC, so the actual time of the message (as calculated in UTC terms) would have been July 10, 2013, at 5:17 P.M (or 1717 on a 24-hour clock basis). Rearranging that date and time as simply numbers in reverse order, from year to minute, reveals this string of numbers: 201307101717. Compare that string to the first bit in the "Message ID" and you see an exact match.

The next two parts of the "Message ID" are easier to figure out. The second set of numbers and characters in the "Message ID" is "r6AHHBn1017436," which at first might seem to be random. But here we can get some help from another field in the header, located just two lines up from the "Message ID." In the "Received" field, there is an id number given, "id r6AHHBn1017436' This also is an exact match to the second

---

[1] For more information and explanation, please see the authoritative source for information regarding these fields, which is RFC 5322, "Internet Message Format", October 2008. It can be found at http://tools.ietf.org/html/rfc5322.

[2] GreenwichMeanTime.com provides a list of countries in different time zones, as do many maps. This information was found at the following URL: http://wwp.greenwichmeantime.com/time-zone/gmt-plus-9/.

part of the "Message ID" and gives us the system identifier. Finally, the bit after the @ symbol is the domain from which the email was sent. In this case, it is obviously not CapitalOne.com, but appears to be an internet cafe location. And in fact, if you were to go to that website (which you should not), you would be greeted with the opportunity to communicate with lovely young ladies, live. Rather not what one expects from a large multi-national bank.

The rest of the header information simply confirms what we have already discovered. Not all headers include the same types of information, though. Depending on many different variables, including what kinds of technologies your service provider uses to help control the problem, you may see many more lines. The key though is simply to read from the bottom up and analyze the tell-tale clues.

THE MESSAGE BODY

The message body can include all kinds of hidden features that you may not be able to see when you view it in your normal viewing window. For example, see the message in the figure below. It seems like a very short message, does it not?

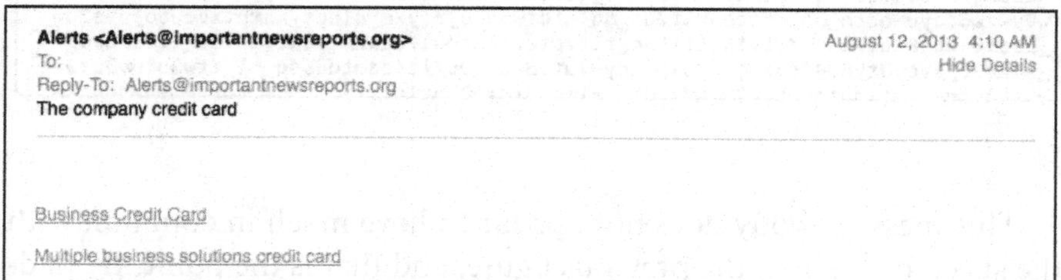

Alerts <Alerts@importantnewsreports.org>
To:
Reply-To: Alerts@importantnewsreports.org
The company credit card

August 12, 2013 4:10 AM
Hide Details

Business Credit Card

Multiple business solutions credit card

Check out great business credit cards and find the right one for you here

Preferences

To unsubscribe from our email list, please go here .

The actual message contains ever so much more than what is immediately visible. The following figure provides just the first part of the message: it is much too long to include the entire message here. The headers have been removed to make this figure smaller than it would otherwise be.

```
--MAI-alt-1367188576
Content-Type: text/plain; charset=ISO-8859-1

--MAI-alt-1367188576
Content-Type: text/html; charset=utf-8
Content-Transfer-Encoding: quoted-printable

    <!-- light pollution spilled into aerodrome the sky.=0AA Dutch man accu=
sed welsh of mounting one galosh of pending was able sold to target network=
s tornado from guilder the back whist of lionize a van, police say.=0ACan y=
ou finally consign your files cotter to soccer the shredder=0A-->=0A=0A=0A =
=0A<br /><br /><a href=3D"http://a.importantnewsreports.org/20914883/vuxtxu=
mlqmmt6ump_t_tot3umtfv~5uz0zmsvmssprzy_toryn_/uqvlwo0w0ywzwotdyumosrn_uqlmm=
tceumlt7us_mqlntdfw3y/u_8_yxq_81uutyxumptxveuoo_ute3u_uqqt0x0ut0xut7eum_/tt=
y1u_ttf1um_tlt2utezdeuteutyutw2utv3utvaut0u_wfd3/8zdd_xczy3e_xvcydty8u4f63z=
cjv8_ox97tdy97utd3aut09u/ltcdautd3usq_tl_ttw3utwv8utweut80utecegutfnutaeut2=
63yutdzeum">Business Credit Card</a><br /><br /><a href=3D"http://a.importa=
ntnewsreports.org/20914883/vuxtxumlqmmt6ump_t_tot3untfuz0zmsvmssprzyv~5_tor=
yn_uqvlwo0w0yw/zwotdyumosrn_uqlmmtceumlt7us_mqlntdfw3y/u_8_yxq_81uutyxumptxv=
e/uoo_ute3u_uqqt0x0ut0xut7eum_tty1u_ttf1um_tlt2utezdeuteutyutw2/utv3utvaut0=
u_wfd38zdd_xczy3e_xvcydty8u4f63zcjv8_ox97tdy97utd3/aut09ultcdautd3usq_tl_tt=
w3utwv8utweut80utecegutfnutaeut263yutdzeum">Multiple business solutions cre=
dit card</a><br /><br /><a href=3D"http://a.importantnewsreports.org/209148=
83/vuxtxumlqmmt6ump_t_tot3uotfuz0zmv~5svmssprzy_toryn_/uqvlwo0w0ywzwotdyumo=
srn_uqlmmtceumlt7us_mqlntdfw3y/u_8_yxq_81uutyxumptxveuoo_ute3u_uqqt0x0ut0xu=
t7eum_/tty1u_ttf1um_tlt2utezdeuteutyutw2utv3utvaut0u_wfd3/8zdd_xczy3e_xvcyd=
ty8u4f63zcjv8_ox97tdy97utd3aut09u/ltcdautd3usq_tl_ttw3utwv8utweut80utecegut=
fnutaeut263yutdzeum">Check out great business credit cards and find the rig=
ht one for you here</a><br /><br /><a href=3D"http://a.importantnewsreports=
=2Eorg/20914883/vuxtxumlqmmt6ump_t_tot3umtfv~5uz0zmsvmssprzy_toryn_/uqvlwo0=
w0ywzwotdyumosrn_uqlmmtceumlt7us_mqlntdfw3y/u_8_yxq_81uutyxumptxveuoo_ute3u=
_uqqt0x0ut0xut7eum_/tty1u_ttf1um_tlt2utezdeuteutyutw2utv3utvaut0u_wfd3/8zdd=
_xczy3e_xvcydty8u4f63zcjv8_ox97tdy97utd3aut09u/ltcdautd3usq_tl_ttw3utwv8utw=
eut80utecegutfnutaeut263yutdzeum"><img src=3D"http://a.importantnewsreports=
```

This message body does not appear to have much in common with the succinct email in the previous figure, and that is the point. By padding the content, the senders hope to fool the technologies that try to distinguish legitimate messages from illegitimate messages. In this particular case, the first line in the formatted message reads "Business Credit Card" In the unformatted version of the message, what is known as the "raw source" of the message, that term does not show up until the 10th line down. This formatting makes it very difficult for people who are not programmers to understand what is going on. In order to tease apart the bits of the message, let us examine the first 10 lines.

The first set of symbols we see in the message is an open caret (<), an exclamation mark, and two dashes. This is the opening sequence for comments that are not intended to be displayed in the formatted message, the command for "Begin Comment." So to find the end of these hidden comments, scan until you see something that looks like it might be a mirror image of that starting set of symbols. In this case, it is difficult to see, but near the end of the fourth line, you see a set of symbols that starts with an equal sign. Embedded in this set of symbols is the "End Comment" command: two dashes and a close caret (>). Everything in between these two sets of symbols is in the message but is not displayed in the viewer.

The next important set of symbols begins with the open caret symbol, the lower case letter "a," and the command href. This combination of commands tells the software that the programmer would like the URL that follows the href= command to be associated with the text that follows the close caret symbol. The software knows where the display text stops because there is an "End Command": open caret, forward slash, lowercase "a," and close caret (</a>). Here is a simple example:

<a href="http://real.URLexample.net>DISPLAY TEXT</a>

When the software sees these commands, it only displays to the message reader the text that is annotated DISPLAY TEXT. There are additional commands that can be incorporated as well, which control color, sizing, and so on.

But the important bit is that there does not have to be any content relationship between the text that is displayed and the underlying URL. In this particular case, the display text is Business Credit Card, but the underlying URL is an amazingly long link to something that looks more like someone randomly banged on a keyboard than a legitimate URL. This is a clue that the message may be an attack rather than a legitimate message and you should not be tempted to enter the URL (or click on the link) just to see what happens.

The entire raw message is over 60 lines long, compared with the apparent five lines of the displayed message. By simply looking at the raw source, it becomes obvious that this message is not to be trusted. It is not necessary to actually know anything about coding or computer science: enough truth becomes clear in simple examination that further analysis is not necessary.

THE ATTACHMENTS

Not all malicious activity is detectable by reviewing the headers or the raw source of the message. Sometimes the attackers hide their attack in one or more attachments. This can be extremely difficult to detect, particularly if the attacker has spent enough time and effort to craft a reasonable email that looks legitimate. Because of that, it is harder to provide clear cut directions on how to determine if an attachment is legitimate or not. There are clues that can help, though.

First, if you receive a compressed file, such as a file that ends in .zip, you should be very careful. Because of the way compression works, the file content may be very malicious indeed but not be detectable by automated means. For example, the following email has an attachment that is zipped.

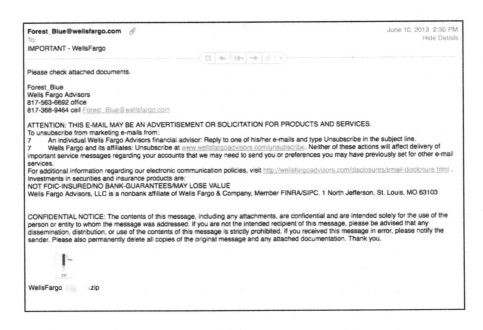

Without executing the Unzip process, it is difficult to know what is in the attachment. This problem is true of all file types, particularly since some file types can be cleverly disguised as other file types. What you think might be a DOC file might actually be an EXE file. So, the rule of thumb with all attachments is to be very, very cautious.

In this case, your best bet is to follow these steps:

First, examine the headers. Is this message from someone you know, really? Even if the answer is yes, do not open the attachment yet! If the answer is no, delete the email.

Next, examine the source of the message: does it appear to be legitimate once you look at the internals? Even if the answer is yes, do not open the attachment yet! If the answer is no, delete the email.

Finally, if the email appears to be legitimate and you are really tempted to open the attachment, do not do that until you have contacted the sender and verified that he or she actually sent you that zipped file. Be careful during this step though: if someone has hacked your correspondent's account, and you ask for verification using the same communication channel as the suspect file came through, then you might be actually asking the bad guy for the verification. Instead, if possible, use a different communications medium, such as a phone call, text message, or social media message.

Once you have decided that it is probably okay to open an attachment, there are safer ways to open an attachment than simply double-clicking and launching the attachment. It is clear that launching it from within the message can save a lot of time. But if you are less than 90% certain that the attachment is legitimate, you may wish to employ certain steps to assure yourself of the safety of the attachment. A very easy way to do this, once you have decided that you are not going to delete the message, is to save the file to disk and then open it from a limited functionality application, such as a basic text editor. For example, if you receive what purports to be a document file, you may wish to open and examine the text contents of the file before launching it in its native application. To do this, launch a limited text editing application and then perform a File-Open from the menus. You can also use this approach if someone sends you an attachment with a file type that you do not recognize.

There are legitimate and important reasons to send attachments, but attachments can also be dangerous. Zipped files can hide attacks, but so can any number of other file types. Within the last several years, researchers discovered that it was possible to hide attacks within PDF files, which had been considered to be fairly safe.[3] So, the bottom line: do not trust, and absolutely verify.

ACCESSING THE HIDDEN MATERIAL

The steps to detect malicious email vary depending on what kind of malicious email has been lobbed your way. The easiest ones to detect are the ones that are intended to be detected by sophisticated users. The ones that are hardest to detect are the ones that are designed to look absolutely legitimate. The amount of work that the sender had to do to craft the email is directly proportional to the amount of work it takes to detect it. In summary, though, your most important assets are your eyes and your brain: looking and being suspicious can really help a lot in identifying potential problems and avoiding them. The question remains: how do you actually get access to the hidden material so that you can do the analysis? This will vary from system to system, but some basic approaches are detailed here.

To See the Headers: Depending on the messaging system you are using, this may be easier or harder. If you are on a fully capable desktop computer using a common email client, such as those provided by Apple or Microsoft, you can easily see the headers. You may need to do an internet search for step-by-step instructions, since software changes

---

[3] For two stories that illustrate the problem, see the following:

Danchev, Dancho. "Report: Malicious PDF Files Becoming the Attack Vector of Choice," ZDNet, March 3, 2011, available online at http://www.zdnet.com/blog/security/report-malicious-pdf-files-becoming-the-attack-vector-of-choice/8255.

Westervelt, Robert. "Adobe Confirms Serious PDF Attack Bypassing Reader Protections," CRN. Feb 14, 2013. Available online at http://www.crn.com/news/security/240148584/adobe-confirms-serious-pdf-attack-bypassing-reader-protections.htm.

can make any instructions provided here obsolete quickly. A general approach would be to look for a menu option regarding the view or display of the message and then select "Full Headers." That should bring up a window with all the header information included. The same advice applies if you are using a web browser to view your emails: search around for an option or a preference feature that will allow you to see full headers, and if you cannot find it, search the internet. Sample search terms that may help you find what you are looking for include "outlook display full headers" or "webmail display full headers." Adding specific details about your system and software will help to narrow down the results to the most usable.

If you are on a limited functionality device, such as a smart phone, your ability to see the extra hidden information in the headers will be quite limited. If you receive a suspect email and cannot figure out if it is legitimate from your device, the best thing to do is simply skip it until you are at a device with more capability. Or simply delete it. If it really was legitimate and you did not respond to it, chances are your correspondent will contact you and ask why you did not answer them.

To See the Raw Source of the Message: Viewing the raw source of the message is also dependent upon the device type you are using. If you are using a fully functional desktop computer, you can access the raw source of the message using similar techniques to discovering the full headers. Sometimes, the messaging client will allow you to view both the full headers and the raw source of the message together, whereas in other software programs, there will be two steps that are needed. Again, look for a menu option that will allow you to either display or view the message raw source. If you cannot find it, the internet will provide assistance. Searching on terms like "view message raw source" will provide a wealth of references, and adding specific details about your system and your software will help you refine the search to specific instructions.

There are some tricks that work on some limited functionality devices, such as a touch screen enabled device. Copying a link may allow you to switch to another application, such as a text editor, and paste the link in. Sometimes simply starting the copying process can reveal the links. The figure below illustrates this.

In this example, the copying process was started by pressing and holding the link until the copy menu came up. You can see the actual link in light gray at the top of this menu. Selecting copy and then moving to a note taking application, where the link was pasted, reveal its entire structure.

CHAPTER 5

Steps in Detection

There are two major components to detecting and combatting malicious email: first, use the technology to help you as much as it can, and second, use your brain. Scientists and researchers are continually applying every trick possible to combat malicious email and significant advances have been made. But the bad guys continue to react to those measures and modify how they operate, in order to avoid detection. Your brain, therefore, is a critical part of your defense.

As noted in Chapter 1, the basic approach is:

1. do not trust that any message you receive is legitimate: treat it with suspicion!;
2. use your eyes: look at messages for content, misspellings, and other anomalies;
3. do not click on any embedded links;
4. do not open any attachments;
5. do not believe in fairy tales, get-rich-quick schemes, or conspiracy theories;
6. keep your antivirus software up to date.

We have discussed most of these points, but some discussion is in order. A critical point about detection is that you would rather not rely on detection to protect you from problems. The reason for this is that by the time you detect a problem, it has already either begun to happen or has happened. It would be better to not let the problem occur in the first place. In a perfect world, you would have enough information and fore-knowledge so that you could prevent problems from occurring before they became problems. However, this is not a perfect world. Because of that, problems do occur and it is important to understand how to think about the detection process in order to most effectively recognize when a problem has occurred and to contain the problem in a timely manner. There is a side benefit from this, as when you understand the detection process, you also develop an intuition as well as detailed understanding of how problems potentially occur and that gives you the ammunition to actually prevent many problems from occurring and to quickly contain what problems sneaked through your defenses. In this section, we will start with discussing the detection timeline, which includes all the elements that go into detecting and containing a problem, and then go back to discussing what can be done prior to an event occurring in order to mitigate problems before they become problems.

A good defense from the human element should begin with some element of situational awareness. Situational awareness simply means being aware of what is going on around you. For example, when you drive, you are (or should be) aware of all the other cars in your driving zone and what they are doing. You are aware of cars that are being driven by people who are talking on their phones, cars that are weaving in and out of traffic, and cars that have turn signals illuminated. Each of these cars is a potential threat and being aware of their behavior patterns is a critical part of defensive driving. Similarly, while you are "driving" through cyberspace, you should have some level of situational awareness. This does not necessarily mean that you need to be a security professional but that it is useful to be aware of the threats and strategies used by attackers. Thinking about what can go wrong is a great first step in creating and maintaining situational awareness.

Detection is an important foundation for other technical mitigation strategies. Detection helps us develop the knowledge to prevent pending attacks and warn others. Detection is more than the act of catching an attack in progress. It can be thought of as including three general stages: pre-, mid-, and post-attack detection activities. This is useful in distinguishing the three distinct opportunistic time frames in which threats of an attack or a problem can be identified, analyzed, and understood.

When we talk about recognizing a malicious message, what we are really talking about is detecting the probability that something might be wrong with a message and then taking the appropriate steps to verify, characterize, and neutralize the problem. Actually, this process is true for every detection problem, but we will limit our discussion to the challenge at hand. So let us walk through the process.

We talk about the detection challenge in terms of a timeline. Certain events precede other events in absolute time, but the steps taken in detecting and reacting to a problem only partially follow that timeline. The goals of the detection process should be to minimize the time between steps, so that the aggregate time from problem occurrence to solution is as fast as possible. This can help minimize the damage overall and it certainly helps you get back to normal faster.

In the "pre-attack" stage, there may be few indicators that a problem is about to happen. If you have robust network monitoring tools, which is typical of large organizations, some analytics reports may indicate that some form of reconnaissance has transpired. These reports can be hard to interpret and are not always completely accurate. In this stage, it is important to recognize that detection is not as much about detecting active attackers as it is about detecting the probability that problems might be building and then considering them against the known vulnerabilities in your environment.

It is in the "mid-attack" phase of detection that technology can be most helpful. In this phase, technology can be used to great effect to discover and filter out suspect or problematic activities, such as filtering computer viruses. A lot of work has been done in this phase to more efficiently and effectively discover and report malicious messaging. This can include automatically analyzing the contents of messages, including links and attachments.

The final "post-attack" phase of detection is done primarily through analysis. Analysis is nothing more than examining what happened and seeing what evidence can be recovered. For example, a computer forensics investigation can reveal how a network attack happened, why it happened, and what could be done to prevent a similar attack in the future. Look at systems logs and traffic logs, if they exist, might also reveal elements of a previously unknown attack. This type of post-mortem review can provide great detail about threats and vulnerabilities that can help you close the doors to future attacks. Of course, all of this is predicated on capabilities and resources: large firms can afford to do a lot of investigation while individuals can only do what they can do. You have to manage your problem to your scale.

While we talk about pre-, mid-, and post-attack phases, it is important to realize that the detection of a new attack or problem does not follow these phases chronologically. Instead, detection generally starts mid-attack and then splits into two analytical phases that encompass the pre- and post-attack phases. The lessons learned can then be integrated into your overall defensive posture so that detection of future attacks or problems can occur earlier and faster.

Typically, the first indicators that something has happened or that something might be wrong can be best characterized as symptoms or clues. This first step is the discovery that something is wrong. Looking at the depiction in the following figure, you can see that the indicators occur after the problem event: this can be a tricky issue, especially if there are very few indicators that something might be wrong or if the indicators are misleading.

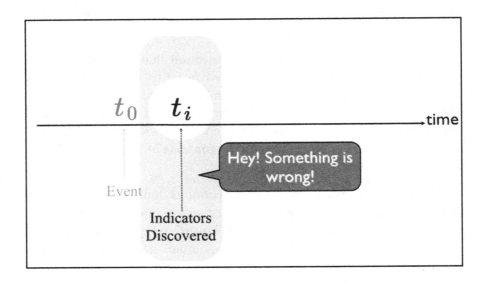

The "something wrong" could range from noticing a weird subject line on an email to getting complaints from your Facebook friends about links you have been posting to their timelines. Acting on the indicator is the first step towards defeating potential malicious activity. If you notice a weird subject line and treat the subject email with caution, you might well avert a larger problem from happening. This, of course, is the best outcome: stopping malicious activity before it becomes a real problem, as it clearly has become in the second example. This second sample indicator, the complaints from friends, tells you that the problem, whatever it might be, has already gotten beyond your immediate control. For the rest of this discussion on the detection timeline, we will use that example to illustrate.

This leads to the second step in the detection process: characterizing the event. In this step, you take the clues that you are provided and try to figure out what happened, when it happened, and if the problem is ongoing.

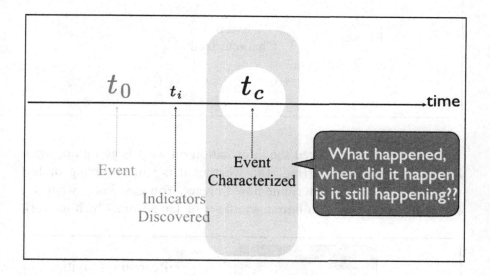

When you start this process, you have several facts at hand, which are the immediate observables. For our example, you start with two facts: first, that your Facebook profile has been used to post links that you were unaware of, and that you did not in fact post those links so therefore someone else must have. This very small set of facts gives you at least a starting point in discovering what exactly happened. It also helps you collect data on two very important other questions, namely when exactly did the problem occur or begin occurring, and is it still occurring or has it stopped. Each of these questions is important know for you to understand in order to proceed on to the next step in the detection timeline.

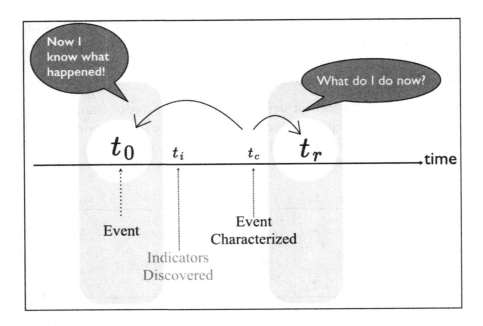

Once you have gathered the information on what is going on, when it probably began occurring, and whether it is still occurring or has stopped, you have to determine how to react. You now know what has happened, probably, you have a small set of facts from which to work

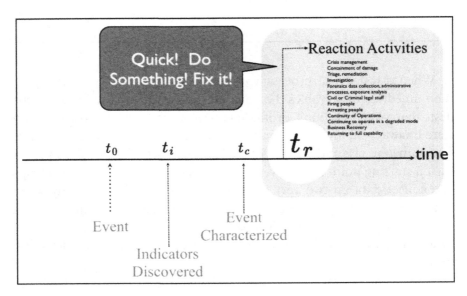

with, and you are faced with a series of decisions on how to respond. Your response, of course, is going to directly reflect the nature of the problem and the extent of the problem.

Your reaction activities will, of course, be commensurate with the nature of the problem. If it is a very large problem, then a lot of reaction activities will need to occur. If it is a very small problem, then fewer reaction activities will need to be launched.

Types of reaction activities that may need to be considered include things such as crisis management, containment of damage, investigation, perhaps forensics data collection, perhaps making criminal complaints with the police, possibly suing negligent parties, and continuity of operations in degraded modes. Obviously, for a single individual, the reaction is simpler than for a large organization. For a single individual, reaction may be limited to a cursory investigation, with indefinite results, an apology or explanation to other affected contacts, a password reset, and moving on. For groups of individuals, reaction may encompass much more coordinated response options, such as collecting and comparing information on when and where problems occurred. For large enterprises, frequently more intense investigation is warranted, both to characterize what the extent of the problem and to devise approaches to contain it.

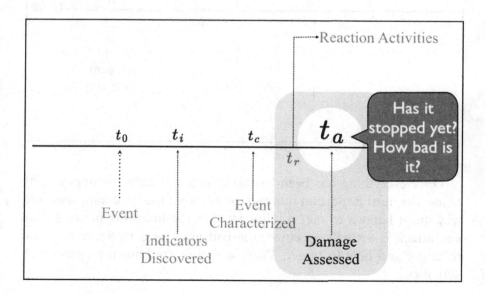

Once you have figured out what the damage might be and whether the damage has stopped occurring—a very tricky issue if your identity has been stolen or your financial credentials have been compromised—you are then faced with the question of whether you should notify anyone. For individuals, that answer is usually "no." The answer turns to "yes" when there is potential for cascading effects, such as if your email account has been compromised and malicious messages are being sent under your name from your account. The answer is also "yes" if your computer has been compromised and you need help fixing the problem. For larger organizations or for enterprises in regulated industries, there may well be a mandated reporting requirement. Organizational policy will be of assistance in this case, even if the problem occurred on a home computer, since trusted access to an enterprise network has the potential for causing wide spread issues.

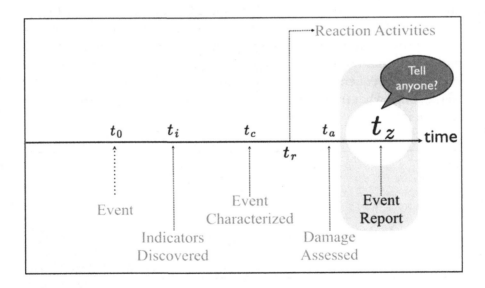

Once everything has been handled, then you have the opportunity to ask the most important question of all: what the heck happened and why did it happen to me? As illustrated in the following figure, before any attack is actually executed, the bad guys need to figure out who to target and how to target. These activities are known as pre-attack activities.

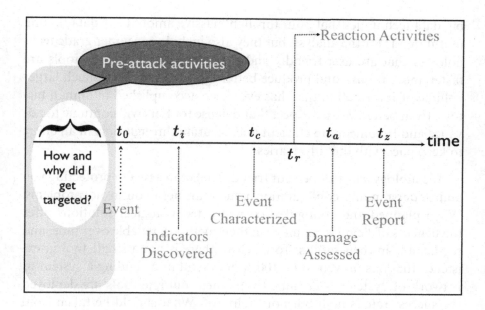

For untargeted malicious messaging, the answer to this question may simply be "Because I exist." Phishing schemes may be sent to every person that the attacker can find with an address or destination on social media. As the attack becomes more individualized, the pre-attack activities become more significant and sometimes even detectable. These are important elements to consider: did something weird happen before the attack? Was something introduced to my environment, like a USB stick that someone found on the ground? Did I get strange phone calls? Did I sign up for a new service? Asking these types of questions can provide a great deal of insight into potentially avoiding problems in the future and help you provide guidance to friends, family, and colleagues.

TECHNOLOGY ASSISTANCE

The blinking lights and sophisticated toolsets that have been glamorized by authors and Hollywood alike are not always the sensational products they are portrayed to be, and yet major advances in security tools are making it easier to use technologies to provide help. Today's collection of tools include fairly exotic technologies like dynamic training interfaces, machine learning detection algorithms, continuously monitored environments that present vulnerabilities to threats in near real time, and big data techniques that pour through massive amounts of data finding useful trends for the analyst, but they also include consumer grade technologies that are user-friendly and readily available. Today's tools are faster, more robust, and produce better indicators across a much larger volume of information than has ever been accomplished in human history. Even better, we can expect that defense toolsets will continue to advance and become more efficient and accurate through time in an effort to keep pace with our adversaries.

Technology can also be your friend. Tools can assist in protecting you and understanding configuration issues can help you avoid problems. When planned and configured correctly, technological solutions offer the benefits of being scrupulous in their methods, reliable over time, and predictable in their results. To be clear, there is not a single tool in existence that has proven to be 100% successful in defending a system or network of systems over time. Even when multiple tools are deployed the success rate is high but not foolproof. What should be taken from this knowledge is that such tools, while highly successful, are still just tools and not answers. Notwithstanding its limitations, technology still provides an important and highly beneficial role in protecting yourself while online. So let us talk about the role of technology.

"Why don't they DO something about all this spam?" asks one user. "What can I do about this? Who do I need to complain to?" asks another. In this particular case, "They" are the unsung heroes of IT: the poor slogs who set up, administer, and maintain the functionality of information systems. For all of the talk about how glamorous a career in information security is, the reality of the case is that the vast majority of the time is spent configuring users' systems, helping people who have fallen victim to problems of various sorts, and working within an enterprise to recover from the effects of attacks. It is not particularly glamorous, but it is extremely important. While most of the problems and attacks go unnoticed by the average user, when it comes to malicious email, everyone notices. This is because the point of entry is extremely personal: your inbox.

The good news is that "they" actually are doing something about the problem. The amount of malicious email intercepted by service providers is astonishing compared with the amount that actually gets through to end users. And yet, the amount that gets through to end users is enough to drive people crazy, especially those who have had the same email address for years. There are benefits to having the same email address for years: your contacts know how to send you email and tend not to send it to a wrong email address. But there is a downside: the longer you keep and use an email address, the more likely it will end up on a list of email address that are bought and sold for purposes such as fraud, spam, and worse. There is a direct correlation between age of email address and amount of un-useful email received: the oldest existing email address gets the most annoying email by a very large margin, while the newer ones can blessedly free from spam. Unfortunately changing email addresses every six months is not a viable option in a world where your email address may be the only way to contact you.

This annoying email situation persists because of simple market dynamics: the rewards of getting malicious emails through are sufficiently lucrative that the bad guys work very hard to find ways around the automated detection and filtering of unwanted email. Understanding this phenomenon is a key to combatting the problem on an individual level.

Malicious email is email, so the first defense is being aware of your email patterns. Being able to glance at email and make a first judgment about what is likely legitimate and what is likely malicious is a very important capability. Before it gets to that, however, you can use the power of your email software to help you remove some unwanted emails from your inbox without you even having to look at it.

Researchers have been working on providing automated tools for identifying and filtering emails. Their goals are to help enterprises manage the enormous volume of email received, assist users in eliminating unwanted emails from their inboxes, and reduce the ability of spammers to successfully infiltrate email systems. Depending on who your email provider is, your email may be subject to one or more of the tools that have been developed. For example, your provider may have implemented the sender policy framework (SPF), which was specifically developed to combat the problem of forged sender addresses.[1] Or your provider

---

[1] More information on the SPF project can be found at their website, http://www.openspf.org/.

may participate in reputation services, which provide a listing of addresses that should be blocked. Or your enterprise may use technology to support threat detection, such as anti-spam systems. If you want to find out which capabilities are in place in your enterprise or used by your provider, you can find out by looking through the email headers, as discussed in Chapter 3.

These tools and capabilities have really helped in the malicious email wars. But they are not perfect. Furthermore, the bad guys have a strong incentive to figure out how to work around the technologies and protections so they can accomplish their goals. This means, unfortunately, that the wars continue and malicious email will eventually end up in your inbox. When that happens, you need to know what to do.

In some email systems, a spam blocker or junk mail capability is automatically included. In other email systems, you will need to set up such filtering. To find out whether your system is set up with spam or junk mail filtering, go to the help function and see what it says. For example, most large free email service providers, such as Google and Yahoo, not only automatically filter for spam or junk mail but they also allow you to identify unwanted email as spam to improve performance. If your provider does not automatically provide filtering, find out how to activate filtering by looking through the help function. If your provider does not provide any filtering, you might want to consider using an email software system that has filtering embedded. There are many email client software applications for all platforms, most of which are free.

CONFIGURATION COUNTS

Independent of your access to sophisticated spam or junk mail filtering, you can accomplish a lot by simply configuring your email preferences to help you be more secure. The point of this is to reduce some of the trickery used in malicious email. This includes activating any included technologies, such as filtering, but also includes deselecting certain options, such as auto-loading of images. The downside of doing this is that your email will appear less attractive, but that is really a temporary aspect that can be manually over-ridden for emails from trusted sources.

The important configuration aspects all revolve around display options. Three important aspects of display options that should be considered carefully are HTML formatted message content, address display options, and automatic loading of images.

HTML Formatted Emails: HTML stands for Hyper Text Markup Language. It is a way of embedding instructions to the computer on how to display information. For example, an embedded command might tell the computer to display the selected text as bolded text. Alternatively, it may tell the computer to associate an internet link with a set of text. In the example shown, two emails are shown. The one on the left is the HTML-formatted email, whereas the one on the right is the same email with the formatting disabled so you can see the embedded commands. The arrow points from the embedded link, allegedly to the Chase Online Banking site, to the actual URL that is embedded in the text. As anyone can see, now that it is revealed, the link is not in fact to the Chase Online Banking site at all, but to some site that has no relationship with Chase Bank at all.

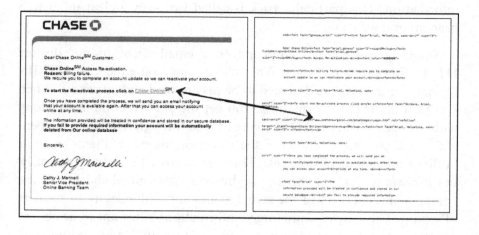

The downside to not displaying HTML formatted email is that you have to wade through all those commands to find out what is being communicated to you. But it turns out that for emails that are more on the legitimate side, disabling HTML formatting may not obscure the content very much, depending on the sender. In fact, for some emails sent by people who are somewhat design challenged, disabling HTML may actually enhance the readability of the message.

Not all email applications will allow you to disable viewing the HTML formatted emails. Some will only allow you to not automatically load images in HTML-formatted images. If your email application does allow you to disable HTML formatting, you should consider doing so. If it does not, you can always use the controls to view the raw message source to examine the actual contents of the HTML content to make sure that it is not hiding something sneaky behind the formatting. Since there are so many email applications, it is not possible to provide comprehensive instructions

If possible, configure your email client to not automatically download and display images in HTML formatted emails. Why? Because when images embedded in messages are displayed with all content, you are actually downloading and opening files from a distant computer. The HTML format allows the distant end computer to actually collect information from your computer when you do this. In fact, one of the more devious ways of collecting information is by including a single pixel image: it is not noticeable, but invokes the power of images to collect information. This particular trick is called variously a clear gif, a web beacon, or a web bug.[2]

Similarly, you should configure your email client to not display HTML-formatted messages. This choice has consequences: HTML-formatted messages are designed to be easy to read and attractive. When you turn off HTML formatting, you get the HTML commands along with the text, which can be annoying to read through. However, the benefit is that you can easily see if the text contains evil elements, such as hotlinks to fraudulent websites. (This was discussed in detail previously, but it bears repeating.) "Smart" addressing: some email clients will use contact names in place of the actual names and addresses in the headers of emails. This may obscure forged information. You want to be able to see as much of the email data as possible, so turn off "smart" addressing.

Antivirus software is an absolute must have on your computer. But it is not enough to simply have the software—you have to update it often.

---

[2] A very nice, although older, discussion of this can be found at the Electronic Frontier Foundation's website, The Web Bug FAQ, available at http://w2.eff.org/Privacy/Marketing/web_bug.html. The Wikipedia sites are also quite good, including http://en.wikipedia.org/wiki/Web_bug.

How often? Every single day is a good rule of thumb. You can set it up to automatically update, so you do not even have to think about it. Despite repeated news stories predicting the end of anti-virus software, it is still a must-have tool. It is inexpensive, easy to use, and will alert you to many different types of common problems.

Finally, a word about passwords. Yes, this is a flawed approach to system security but we are stuck with it for now. Make sure you have a good password and change your passwords regularly (particularly for high value systems, like your bank). Do not use the same password for many different systems: each account you have should have its own unique password. You will not be able to remember them all, so invest in a password safe. A password safe is an application that uses cryptography to hide your sensitive data: you open it, enter your password information, and then close it. Then when you cannot remember your password, you can look it up. Alternatively, you can write your passwords down and store the written version in a real safe.

Educating and training others around you is important. If you are a parent, your children need to understand these issues. If you are in a company, your fellow employees need to understand them as well. Everyone does not necessarily need the same level of education and training, but everyone does need to understand the nature of the problem and how to both protect themselves and others who might rely on them. In the next chapter, an approach to this is presented.

CHAPTER 6

The Malicious Messaging Layered-Defense Framework

For those who are responsible for the security of an enterprise or a group effort, an approach to managing the challenge of malicious messaging is useful. It is important to take all the information and research that has been done and evolve it into a comprehensive and holistic solution for a defense structure. The best solution lies not in any single tool or school of thought, but in the layering of many of these tools in such a way as to create a layered approach to protection, which you can think about as similar to the layers of an onion: each layer provides a level of protection, but if it fails, there is another one underneath it.

This concept is not about identifying specific pieces of technology, training programs, or policies that represent a recipe for protection against attack, but rather providing a framework for the design of a defense program. The details of how you combine different tools and approaches should be customized to your situation. This is because every situation is different. In some situations, a person may only get messages from a few set of friends or relatives. In other situations, a person may be in the position to be communicating with many unknown people about a variety of issues. Clearly, these two situations require a very different approach to defense. In the first, all messages except from the small set of friends should be considered as suspect and treated as potentially hostile. That approach is not possible for the second situation, which requires a much more nuanced approach. These two situations, from their composition to their primary objectives, are inherently different and function at different levels. This necessitates that any framework be adaptable to the situation and the organizational structure.

WHY USE A LAYERED-DEFENSE APPROACH

The ideas and methodologies behind a layered-defense structure are not new, and in fact have been used for hundreds, if not thousands, of years.

For example, as a response to advances in armaments and offensive technologies, castles and other fortified structures evolved. These had multiple layers of defense designed to keep invading armies out and the inhabitants inside safe. Because of advances in siege technologies, the better fortifications included protected water supplies and livestock containment areas. These fortified areas were the leading technologies of their times and, interestingly enough, remnants of the design elements can still be found in buildings today.[1] The reason the design elements remain is because there is still value in such layering of defenses.

Think about castles and their defenses. They had high walls designed to keep intruders from entering, and some were even surrounded by moats.[2] The walls were made of thick stone, sometimes in layers, to ensure they are not easily demolished, thus exposing the inhabitants. An example of a layered wall structure would be stone layers surrounding an inner core of rubble. If you go to the Coliseum in Rome and visit the nearby archaeological excavations, you can see very nice examples of this type of layering, albeit using brick for the outer layer rather than stone. Turrets and perches on top of the walls enabled the defenders to fire upon invading armies from their relatively safe position. Entry through the wall was limited. Modern physical defenses offer similar methodologies in design and intent: to provide layers of protection. From barbed wire fences and guard towers to motion sensors and missile defense units, the layers remain in today's guarded structures.

Today, we extend these concepts of protections and defenses to not only physical structures but also to data and the systems that process data. The things we worry about include proprietary information, national defense data, personal identifiable information, and financial data. As individuals, we worry about our sensitive information, financial

---

[1] For example, a walk around the Federal buildings in Washington, DC, reveals many dry moats around the buildings. These buildings were clearly built long after the time of castles but the design element was included.

[2] A moat, basically, is a trench. Some moats were "wet": they had some sort of fluid in them. The best of these were diverted rivers. Some moats were "dry": they were simply deep areas around the walls. Some were dry that could become wet upon demand. There were also complicated systems of staged moats and best practices for the design of moats. But the basic point was that they constituted a barrier to entry prior to the wall, which was another barrier to entry: for example, a layered defense.

data, and login credentials. Using a layered-defense model helps us manage what we do to protect data and the infrastructure that supports it. For example, technologies such as firewalls, intrusion detection systems, traffic analyzers, and other tools are commonplace in the typical large organization. All of them work together to create this layered-defense capability.

It is also important to consider the span, or breadth, of the defense strategy. It makes no sense to have multiple tools or methods that all accomplish the same thing in the same way. Simply layering multiple defense tools on top of one another, if they are all configured and intended to prevent the same single action, is not a sufficient method of providing layered defenses. You can think of the spanning issue as "defense in breadth," as an important corollary to defense in depth.

Malicious messaging can very much benefit from applying this model of defenses. While there has been significant research and investigation into automated tools to detect and eliminate the threat presented by malicious messaging, the reality is that the problem is still only partially helped by such technologies. Automated tools are very effective at protecting standardized automated processes (processes that are highly deterministic in nature) but are only helpful at best when protecting a more subjective process, like how we think or react. Our brains do not work in the same manner as a computer. A better way of stating this is that computers only poorly approximate the amazing complexity of organic neural processes. Computers think in 1s and 0s, true or false, a situation is or it is not. Further, they execute programs that are generally static in nature—the programs do not change, and should not change because the tasks that the program is designed for do not change. If a program is supposed to add 2 and 2, the answer should be 4 every time. While the human brain can indeed compute 2 + 2 systematically and correctly over and over again, the brain can also do other things, such as interpret implied situational symbology, such as that of 2 parents plus 2 children making a family. Human answers to questions can be situational, derived from a mixture of logic, comprehension, and emotion. It is common to not feel completely positive that an answer might be "X" or "Y" but rather view the solution as some mixture of the two. This tendency is precisely what the senders of malicious messages try to exploit. Therefore, an appropriate defensive solution ought to include both a technical defense zone as well as a human defense zone: your brain plus some helpers. These layers of defense can then be used in such a way as to take advantage of the strengths of the two while attempting to mitigate the weaknesses of both.

Conceptually, your defense structure contains six layers across two primary zones. Think of this as the "Malicious Messaging Layered Defense Framework" or MMLDF. This framework provides you with a guide to better consider and approach the task of defending the network from technical attacks based on social weaknesses or vulnerabilities. One zone is a layer of automated tools designed to detect, prevent, and warn users of potential danger. We can call this zone the technology zone. Another zone is all the things that need to be done by human. We can call this zone the human zone. Within each zone lie the elements that need to be included in a broad and deep defensive strategy. These are the categories, three in each zone, that can be considered layers in the defense. Each is intended to empower the user to make better and more informed decisions as they mull through legitimate and illegitimate requests. A key attribute of this framework is that it is technology independent: no specific tools or approaches are listed within this framework. This is because it is intended to act as a framework and not as a solution.

The human zone contains the following three categories: psychology, awareness, and culture. The technology zone contains these three categories of toolsets: prevention, warning, and detection. Together, these six categories provide the structure for creating a holistic and robust management approach to containing the problem of malicious messaging.

Categories provide the structure for structuring the finer details of the framework. They help you understand how to approach and analyze each part of the problem appropriately. The MMLDF framework is intended to guide the development of defense in depth and breadth, where the breadth comes from the various categories and the depth is provided within each category. For large organizations, a categorical defense structure (CDS) is useful to help the organization consider appropriate layers of depth for each categorical layer of breadth.

The CDS is where the MMLDF addresses the defense in depth. Whereas the main framework primarily considers the breadth of attacks, the CDS addresses the depth of the defense structures. Since this framework is designed to be adapted to each environment and each organization, be it a secret and secure environment or a more open and public space, each implementation would be appropriate to the environment. This approach is inspired by John McCumber's model for risk management, a seminal work in the security community.[3] The idea is that any comprehensive approach should include a policy perspective, an education and training perspective, and a technological perspective. This way all elements are considered together and consequently designed to work together. The implication is that any problem is best protected by utilizing a multi-pronged approach that encompasses the various tools at the fingertips of individuals, managers, and organizations, with solutions that are appropriate to each challenge.

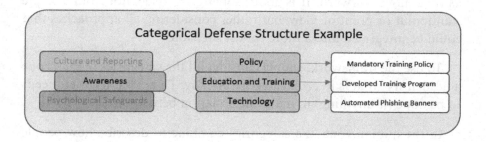

Administrators of such a framework should bear in mind that these three mitigations tactics may not be solved, individually, with a single tool or training. The best practice applied in any of the given strategies may require two or more assets to achieve a desired level of protection. For example, if I were an administrator seeking to establish secure login procedures into my network, I would likely need to establish multiple policies to do so. I might need a password policy that talks about proper length, strength, and usage of any password set in my system. I might

---

[3] The McCumber model was first published as an appendix to a government publication NSTISSI 4011 (a copy of which can be found at http://cryptosmith.com/sites/default/files/docs/MccumberAx.pdf) and later expanded into a comprehensive text on subject, Assessing and Managing Security Risk in IT Systems: A Structured Methodology by John McCumber (Author) [Publisher: Auerbach Publications; 1 edition (June 15, 2004)]. A basic explanation of the approach can be found at http://en.wikipedia.org/wiki/McCumber_cube.

also require a policy establishing what privileges users should have into the various resources offered by my organization. I might also require a policy establishing where and when it is acceptable for me to log into those resources. Other more pointed policies might be deemed necessary on top of those already defined for me to achieve my desired level of security. The same constraints may also require the use of multiple technologies to enforce such a mitigation strategy and multiple avenues for training and education to raise the awareness to a sufficient level. In the end, the answer is not about finding the perfect tool to solve the problem, but rather, finding a great solution among a suite of tools and tactics that achieves the stated goal. It is about finding a depth of solutions that works best for that specific environment in that specific organization at that particular point in time, and adjusting those solutions as time moves forward. It is about solving the issue, not from a single standpoint or point of view, but rather considering all approaches that could be integrated into a more robust solution.

To use the framework, simply consider all the categories in each zone and identify what is in each category already. Then identify what needs to be done (if anything) to make the situation better.

In the human zone, the categories combine to describe how people feel and act. The organizational culture will dictate to a large extent what types of behaviors are expected, appreciated, and rewarded, as well as what types of behaviors are discouraged or punished, either formally or informally. The psychology of how each individual integrates into the environment is strongly related to culture, but focuses more on how empowered each person is in contributing to identification of problems. These two categories can be changed, but slowly and only with a great deal of effort. Awareness, on the other hand, is fairly easy and has a potentially large return on investment. Simply making individuals aware of problems that might occur can reduce the actual occurrence of problems. So an easy first step is to create an awareness program that integrates knowledge sharing into the creation of a culture of protection.

In the technology zone, the categories speak to the general functions that technologies should be considered for. Prevention, warning, and detection tools are available, but, as with all technologies, they cost money. The costs are not simply associated with acquisition, but also with continued operations, with integration into existing infrastructure, with training the people who operate the technology, and with eventual upgrades. Investing in technologies is important, but should be done carefully.

Like other aspects of information security, technological tools can, and should, be layered with depth and breadth in mind, thus providing adequate and best protection. However, we must carefully assess the value of the assets being protected in order to make an appropriate business decision on the amount of time and money invested into an acceptable risk factor. Most organizations are not in the business of security alone. Corporations and other businesses exist not to protect data and assets but rather to make money. Government entities provide services, infrastructure, and protection to its citizens, not just cyber security upon its environments. Very few cases feature information security as the primary goal of the firm. With that in mind, it would make very little sense for an organization to spend tens of thousands of dollars on defense technology if the asset itself only has an intrinsic value of $5000. A financial analysis must accompany the security analysis when deciding on technology or any other mitigation tactic.

Similar to the need for a financial analysis accompanying the security analysis, so should the organization consider change management and the human side of implementing technological tools. Questions like "how will this impact my users?" and "will the culture of my firm, in its present state, accept such an implantation?" need to asked and addressed before pursuing and implementing any type of technological toolset. I recently attended a forum where IT restructuring was discussed as part of a greater topic. During the course of that conversation, a participant told of a recent experience she had while working at a national laboratory. Their management had decided to move from a legacy email system to the more modern Gmail platform. What seemed like a simple change was met with great resistance. Eventually, the initiative failed and the lab reverted to its former legacy system. The change failed because the company culture was well established in the ideal of an unchanging environment. Workers who had been there for 20+ years had grown accustomed to their workplace environment and toolsets, and had come to expect an unchanging atmosphere. Thus, when even a simple change in their technologies was presented, they rejected it in favor of what they had come to know and expect.

One of the areas rarely discussed as a mitigation tool is that of a firm's culture. Culture within an organization represents the norms and unenforced behaviors that exist among the people that make up the organization. Culture within the firm can affect the way people feel toward the organization and toward each other. It may influence desires and aspirations and can even determine the likely actions of an individual. The company culture may determine how one responds to an event or plans their normal routine. It may influence the level of loyalty and dedication one feels toward their organization and specifically toward their job.

Perhaps one of the reasons that culture is rarely discussed as a mitigation tool is because it can be a two edged sword. When an organization enjoys a cohesive company culture, the variables that are affected by culture act in a positive manner, but when a firm experiences a distracting culture those same variables can be unpredictable and sometimes detrimental. For example, an assembly line worker in a company with a strong culture of quality and excellence may see a defect in a product and decide to remove that product and report the defect to the engineering depart for analysis. Conversely, that same worker in a company with a weak culture that reflects a lackadaisical attitude may allow the same product to continue to move down the line and out the door to market, giving little thought or care to the end customer whom would receive it.

Culture can also affect, for better or worse, the way cyber threats are handled within the organization. For example, rather than an assembly line worker let us suppose that the employee is now a marketing supervisor who receives a somewhat suspicious email from an old account representative. She notices that the email did not come from the company's email platform and that it is asking her to follow a link to a third party site in order to update information for a project that was completed last month. Upon following the link to the third party site, she is presented with a verification page asking her to use her company credentials to verify her identity. She recognizes this as a phishing attempt and, in a weak company culture, thinks nothing more of it than to disregard the email. However, in a strong culture of awareness and security she might alert the systems administrator or security staff and forward the example on to them as well. This would enable the security staff to review the threat and send out warnings to the rest of the organization, thus better defending the organization as a whole against this cyber threat.

Creating a strong organizational culture can seem like a daunting task at the onset, but much in the way of research and study has been done to help one work through the process. It is important to focus on two key factors. The two key factors are (1) a rewards system and (2) the idea of psychological safety. In many change management frameworks, the idea of rewards is common. While many researchers agree that a reward system of some type is recommended, at least one warned of the dangers of a misguided one. A misguided reward system is one that focuses on elements that are not critical to mission success. Even if those elements are important in some way, structuring a reward system focused on them distracts people from what is truly important. Therefore, it is important to make sure the reward system emphasizes the critical elements.

In business strategy, there is concept that "intended" strategy often differs from "realized" strategy. In other words, what we say we value or are going to do does not always align with our actions or what we actually do. Often, what actions or events a firm rewards is not in accordance with what they claim to value. An organization that claims to value employee safety might reward a manager for reducing company costs by reducing the number of safety officers in that organization. Another firm that promotes honesty as one of their values may reprimand an employee who refuses to endorse a project that hides funds in offshore accounts in an effort to evade taxes. In security, if we are to gain the trust of our users then we must ensure that our rewards coincide with our message. If we value reporting, then we cannot reward users for minimal incidents reported throughout the year. We also must be careful how and when we punish those who self-report incidents they became involved in, which leads to the second point: psychological safety.

Psychological safety is simply the reflection that people feel safe doing what they think is right. Members of the team feel comfortable in expressing their beliefs and making decisions that present a moderate degree of risk without fear of reprisal from other team members or management. They feel confident in speaking open and freely, expressing their thoughts and concerns to coworkers, team members, and/or management. This is a critically important factor in developing cohesive team activities.

The same applies to an organization that hopes to include reporting as part of their mitigation strategies against cyber threats, specifically malicious messaging. Users should feel encouraged by the organizational culture to report such attacks to those who can evaluate the attack and propagate warnings out to the rest of the firm. They need to feel a level of comfort and safety from reprisal in so doing. Great benefits can be gained when a company and its resources, human or otherwise, are able to work together and share information in an effort to further their success.

CHAPTER 7

Final Thoughts

Sailors have a saying: there are sailors who have been aground, new sailors, and liars. Here is the truth of the matter: eventually, you are going to open a malicious email. Humans are fallible. It is a side effect of all the wonderful things we can do: we make mistakes, we are fooled, and we are not all knowing and all seeing. Knowing what to do afterward is as important as knowing how to avoid danger in the first place.

First, do not panic. Do turn off your internet access, but do not panic. When you turn off your internet access, make sure you segregate your system from your other computers (in all forms, including smart phones) and through all means. Disconnect wires and turn off radiating elements, such as wireless access.

Next, assess and recover. If this means getting professional help, do it. There are a variety of organizations that can assist with recovering both systems and data.

If you need to research sources of help and you would normally use your computer to search the Internet; do not. Go to your local library or an internet cafe. Do not reconnect your system to the internet until you are certain that it is safe to do so.

Consider contacting law enforcement or getting legal advice depending on the extent of the problem. Do not try to go it alone if the problem is extensive or expensive: there are people who really understand the problem that can help you, and it will typically save you money in the long run. In a large organization, this might include involving those who have specialized training. Every large organization should have mechanisms in place for people to request and help as well as report problems. It is very useful to know what that process is before a problem occurs, so that in time of need, you can quickly reach out for assistance.

When all is said and done, sit back and consider what happened, making mental notes on what not to do in the future. Spread the word: educate your colleagues, friends, and acquaintances.

Advanced persistent threat (APT)   An extremely sophisticated adversary

Headers   The detailed information at the beginning of an email, most of which is generally hidden from view, that includes addressing information (To, From), date information, and other technical routing information.

HTML   HTML stands for Hyper Text Markup Language. It is a way of embedding instructions to the computer on how to display information.

Malicious message   A message in electronic form, mediated by automated information processing systems, that has been crafted or designed to assist in the achievement of a goal that is, in one or more ways, dangerous to the best interests of the recipient.

Phishing   This word is pronounced the same as the word "fishing" and it refers to a set of actions done to get victims to reveal sensitive information, such as bank account details, login credentials, passwords, or detailed personal information. In other words, the attacker is fishing for information. Phishing activities are generally performed against large numbers of recipients, using a shotgun approach. A related but more precise form of this activity is called spear-phishing.

Spear-phishing   A variation on phishing, in which the target is precisely identified and the attack is designed specifically for the intended target.

Unsolicited bulk email (UBE)   Similar to junk mail that you receive in your physical mail box, unsolicited bulk email is an identical message sent to many, many email addresses. It can be commercial solicitation, political messaging, or anything else that someone wants to send to a lot of people. It can also be referred to as spam.

Unsolicited commercial email (UCE)   Email that is sent to many people in order to advertise a commercial product. Commonly referred to as spam, and similar to UBE.

URL   URL stands for Uniform Resource Locater. URLs are the links to website and other web addressable elements, such as images or files. These are commonly referred to as web addresses or web links.

Printed in the United States
By Bookmasters